Economic Reforms *Sans* Development

OTHER BOOKS BY THE SAME AUTHOR

SOME PROBLEMS OF UNDEREMPLOYMENT

AGRICULTURAL ECONOMIC THEORY AND THE INDIAN ECONOMY
(jointly with Prof. J.R. Bellerby)

MONEY, BANKING AND ECONOMICS DEVELOPMENT IN ZAMBIA
(jointly with Dr. J.B. Zulu, former Governor, Bank of Zambia)

MONEY, SAVING AND ECONOMIC DEVELOPMENT

FINANCIAL SYSTEM FOR INFORMAL SECTOR
(jointly with Dr. V.D. Lall)

THE NEW ARCHITECTURE OF THE RURAL CREDIT SYSTEM

FINANCIAL SECTOR REFORMS AND INDIA'S ECONOMIC DEVELOPMENT,
(a set of two volumes, Academic Foundation, 2002)

DR. N.A. MUJUMDAR is former Principal Adviser, Reserve Bank of India. At present he is the Editor of the Indian Journal of Agricultural Economics and also Honorary Professor at the Society for Development Studies.

Dr. Mujumdar began his career as Lecturer in what was then known as the School of Economics, University of Bombay. He was Nuffield Fellow of Oxford University, Oxford, in 1959, and after his return to India, joined the Reserve Bank of India.

Dr. Mujumdar has also worked, under the auspices of the International Monetary Fund, as Adviser to the Central Banks of five countries: Zambia, Mauritius, Tanzania, Belize and Cambodia. He was Consultant to FAO, ESCAP and the World Bank. He was member of various Working Groups appointed by the Reserve Bank of India and the Planning Commission.

He has published eight books and a number of research papers in various technical journals.

Economic Reforms *Sans* Development

N.A. Mujumdar

ACADEMIC FOUNDATION
NEW DELHI

First Published in 2004 by

ACADEMIC FOUNDATION

4772-73 / 23 Bharat Ram Road, (23 Ansari Road),
Darya Ganj, New Delhi - 110 002.
INDIA.

Phones : 23245001, 02, 03, 04.
Fax : +91-11-23245005.
e-mail : academic@vsnl.com
www : academicfoundation.com

Economic Reforms Sans Development
N.A. Mujumdar
ISBN 81-7188-357-5

Designed and typeset by Italics India, New Delhi
and printed at Print Perfect, New Delhi.

To my grand-daughter

Sharvari

CONTENTS

III

Banking and Savings

IV

Utilisation of Forex Reserves

V

Crisis of Capitalism

VI

Fiscal Policies

VII

Hunger, Poverty and Rural Development

Introduction

The Introduction to my previous book *Financial Sector Reforms and India's Economic Development* opens with the following sentence: "The financial sector reforms introduced in the 1990s, as part of the process of liberalisation and globalisation of the Indian economy have, in effect succeeded in alienating the financial system from the business of development". The present book enlarges the scope of this central theme by encompassing the whole range of economic reforms – not just financial sector reforms – and seeks to demonstrate that these reforms have resulted in shifting the focus of macroeconomic policy away from the end-objectives of development, namely, reduction in poverty and improvement in the quality of the life of the bulk of the population.

The emphasis of reforms seems to be on exhibiting the form of the text-book characteristics of a liberalised, and open economy, at the cost of the substance of development: reduce State intervention and involvement in economic activities, usher in market-driven economy, abolish all subsidies including food and interest rate subsidies to the poor, and let the poor fend for themselves and so on. In the hierarchy of priorities of contemporary Indian policy makers, for instance, privatisation has gained ascendancy over poverty reduction. Economic reforms have thus become empty rhetorics so far as the attainment of end-objectives of development is concerned.

The bunch of 33 selected articles brought together in this book seeks to provide concrete evidence in support of this central theme. The discussion also sketches the broad contours of policy correctives that are needed if the substance of development is to be retained as an important ingredient in the macroeconomic policy mix.

The discussion in the book is organised around seven aspects: Macro Perspectives of Growth, Monetary and Credit Policies, Banking and Savings, Utilisation of Forex Reserves, Crisis of Capitalism, Fiscal Policies and Hunger, Poverty and Rural Development.

This book should, hopefully, serve as a corrective to the current euphoria about the state of the economy, what with the Finance Minister waxing eloquent on the slogan "We have never had it so good". Admittedly, this slogan is not exactly irrational exuberance because the fundamentals of the economy apparently point to a buoyant economy. On the external front, the country's foreign exchange reserves have already crossed $ 100 billion mark. Exports continue to be buoyant. During April-July 2003, export growth was 9.2 per cent, close on the heels of a 10 per cent growth recorded during the previous year. The mood regarding foreign direct investment (FDI) continues to be upbeat. The rupee has been firming up against the US dollar.

On the domestic front, although 2002-03 was a year of severe drought, the availability of foodgrains was not affected, thanks to the embarrassingly high level of stocks of foodgrains with the Food Corporation of India (FCI). Foodgrains production dipped to 182.6 million tonnes in 2002-03 because of the drought and yet foodgrains stocks with FCI continued to remain at a high level of 36.2 million tonnes in February 2003. Since the monsoon during the current year is very good, foodgrains production may exceed the record level of 212 million tonnes reached in 2001-02, so that foodgrains stocks may swell in 2003-04 to the previous record of 65 million tonnes. It is these stocks which have helped contain inflation. Notwithstanding the severe drought, the underlying inflation rate, represented by the 52 week moving average of the Whole-Sale Price Index (WPI) was 3.3 per cent in 2002-03, as compared to the corresponding figure of 3.6 per cent in the preceding year. The subdued trend in inflation has persisted during the current year. There has been recovery in industrial production during the current year and with the anticipated high growth in agricultural production, national income (GDP) growth may exceed 6.5 per cent. Given this constellation of macroeconomic indicators, no wonder that the Finance Minister is exuberant.

This book poses the question: how far is this exuberance justified? The point is that there is a whole bunch of issues of development as important as the macroeconomic indicators discussed above, which remains unaddressed. This unaddressed agenda includes basic issues like elimination of hunger, and promotion of social development through use of the so-called "surplus" foodgrains, removal of infrastructure constraints by utilisation of surplus foreign exchange resources, strengthening household sector savings by correction of ill-conceived and distorted interest rate and fiscal policies, and redefining the role of banks and financial institutions in the process of development. The crux of the matter is that the redefinition must address India-specific situations. Attempts to develop the capital market, following the IMF/World Bank theology, have been a heroic failure and perhaps development banks need to be resurrected. Public sector banks should enhance their presence in the rural sector with a view to facilitating decentralised development and growth of the non-farm sector. Employment, particularly rural employment, has received a set-back during the reform era and since employment holds the key to tackle poverty and hunger, employment intensive growth should be our objective in future.

The most conspicuous evidence of Indian policy makers' dependence on received wisdom and failure to address India-specific issues is the mountain of "surplus" foodgrains, the size of which had soared to 64 million tonnes at one point of time. The co-existence of embarrassingly huge stocks of foodgrains with distressingly large unsatisfied demand for foodgrains is symptomatic of failure of economic reforms. Indian policy-makers have not covered themselves in glory in this area.

Of course, the size of the mountain has shrunk to 32 million tonnes now because of the drought year 2002-03 but with the bumper harvest in the offing in 2003-04, the stocks may swell again to 60 million tonnes. Yet, precious little has been done to utilise these massive surpluses productively. It is not as if the mountain erupted suddenly, taking the policy makers by surprise. Foodgrain stocks with the public sector rose to 29 million tonnes in 1999-2000 – well above the buffer stock norm of 21 million tonnes and have since been rising consistently. India is the abode of the largest number of under-fed and under-nourished people in the world. According to food and agricultural organisation (FAO), more than 225 million Indians remain chronically undernourished and the UNDP estimates that over half of all Indian pre-schoolers suffer from malnutrition.

How did the policy makers respond to this situation? In an over-zealous attempt to cut food subsidies, Government of India has been raising issue prices of foodgrains distributed through the public distribution system (PDS) and consequently the off-take of foodgrains from the PDS has shown a decline. Foodgrains are thus increasingly becoming inaccessible to the poor. This has led to the swelling of stocks with FCI.

Indian policy makers brought up on the diet of the market theology of IMF and World Bank fault the minimum support price (MSP) system for rice and wheat, for the bulge in food stocks. These experts fail to recognise that the so-called "surplus" foodgrains is only an effective demand surplus and not a genuine surplus in the sense of say, wheat surpluses in the USA. In fact, in the decade of economic reforms, the 1990s, agricultural growth decelerated sharply. The per capita availability of cereals actually declined from 450 grams per day in 1991 to 395 grams in 2001. Even modest projections of demand for cereals in 2020 place the estimate at 260 million tonnes, as compared to the level of 187 million tonnes in 2001. The enormous gap between demand and supply is thus obvious.

Other proponents of the market philosophy make a plea for the abolition of the public distribution system itself, to save the Government from the embarrassment of huge stocks. This is like throwing away the baby with the bath water. Public memory is proverbially short, but at least economists should recall that the emergence of PDS itself was in response to the rapacious nature of private trade in foodgrains, under which both farmers and consumers were exploited through the mechanism of artificially depressing foodgrains prices in the immediate post-harvest period and raising them to unusual heights in the lean season. Whatever may have been the inefficiencies of FCI, it has emerged as an effective counter-veiling force to private trade.

At a time when most Indian policy makers are basking in the reflected glory of the market theology of IMF and World Bank, it is gratifying to note that there are occasional saner counsels. The High Level Committee on Long Term Grain Policy has expressed the view that: given the fact that India accounts for about 15 per cent of world consumption, that world production and trade in grains are highly disturbed, that the vulnerability of the Indian poor is high, policies to encourage and assist the production and distribution of foodgrains, especially cereals, remain integral to the development strategy of the country. One hopes that these wiser counsels will prevent the dismantling of the institutions of minimum support price and public distribution system.

One needs to go further. In this India-specific unique situation it seems feasible to eliminate hunger first, and poverty later. Analytically, this is an important step towards evolving what might be described as "the second best" solution. Conventional wisdom stipulates that the problem of poverty can be tackled through higher GDP growth, expansion of employment, and, additional generation of income in secondary occupations and so on. But this process is a long haul and may take at least two decades, as the recent experience of China has demonstrated. In contrast, this approach of eliminating hunger by using surplus foodgrains meets the test of "immediacy" because we have the where-withal to achieve the objective. How does one go about utilising productively the stocks of foodgrains? A number of modalities are available, including linking of rural development works like micro watershed development programmes to utilisation of foodgrains, instituting a "Grain Loans Facility" for all institutions involved in financing rural development programmes like rural cooperatives, RRBs and even NGOs. Also, there is a need to activate the mid-day meal schemes to provide children in government and government assisted primary schools with prepared meals. This scheme confers multiple benefits on the economy. The rate of literacy is only 60 per cent in India, as compared to China's rate of 81 per cent. Productive utilisation of the mountain of surplus foodgrains is one of the biggest problems facing the economy today. If there is a separate Ministry to deal with disinvestment, why should there not be a separate Ministry for utilisation of surplus foodgrains? The primordiality of the objective of eliminating hunger should subsume all other development objectives.

The same story of failure to utilise surpluses holds true in respect of the country's foreign exchange reserves which have already soared to $ 100 billion. What is the response of Reserve Bank of India (RBI) to this affluence in forex resources? RBI has liberalised foreign exchange allowances for travel, education, medical treatment and so on. Indian corporates and residents can invest abroad and NRIs can repatriate the proceeds of sale of their assets in India. It is as if we are reaching the point of total capital account convertibility. RBI seems to be keen to shed these embarrassingly high level of reserves. The point is that there is an optimum level of forex reserves which the country should maintain to sustain confidence in the economy and currency. It is wasteful to permit accumulation of reserves well beyond this level. For instance, if we assume that the optimum level to be equivalent to the value of say, six months' imports, around $ 30 billion of reserves could be regarded as prudent. Maintaining reserves far in excess of that level is wasteful because the returns on these reserves invested in developed countries like the US, UK and Germany are the lowest, particularly in the present context when the world is passing through the low interest rate regime. Frittering away these valuable resources through liberalising remittances or outflow generally, as the RBI seems to be doing now, is not the appropriate answer. In fact, this approach is reminiscent of the frittering away by India of the huge sterling balances in the Post-War period. Such liberalising of exchange regulations provide another instance of reforms *sans* development. Instead, one could think in terms of using surplus reserves to remove infrastructure constraints: for instance, power is acting as a major constraint on industrial growth. Why not import some power plants to ease the situation? Constructive use of excess reserves could raise the productive capability of the economy.

Historically, the Planning Commission has been crying hoarse that availability of foodgrains and foreign exchange are acting as a major constraint on growth. When these constraints are removed finally, why are the contemporary policy-makers unable to exploit the situation to accelerate GDP growth and enhance the welfare of the bulk of the population? One begins to wonder whether this is because these issues do not find a place in the IMF/World Bank theology.

In India, unlike in the developed countries, the main impetus to overall savings comes from the household sector. Small savings is an important component of household sector savings. Economic reforms have stunted the growth of small savings by reducing the yields on small savings because of the low interest rate regime. The collapse of the Unit Trust of India (UTI) was the mother of all betrayals of the small investor, because both the Government of India and RBI were involved in the management of UTI. In terms of fiscal policy, there was discrimination against bank deposits and in favour of equity: interest income was and is subject to tax. Both the avenues of investment should enjoy a level playing field. India, is one of the few developing countries that can boast of a high savings rate and these distortions in fiscal and interest rate policies need to be corrected, if the high rate is to be sustained and raised further as stipulated in the Tenth Five- Year Plan.

Again, inspired by the IMF, Indian policy-makers have begun to de-emphasise development banks and attempt to develop the capital market. In the process they have decimated, by misconceived policies, the Industrial Development Bank of India (IDBI) which has had an excellent track record. There was a time when many countries used to send their experts to study the IDBI profile so that it can be replicated in their own countries. Thanks to economic reforms, IDBI is in a moribund state today. It is gratifying to note that the Parliamentary Committee has stipulated that in its new *avatar* – converted into a bank – it should retain its development character. With all the rhetoric and the various artificial props given to boost the capital market – like throwing open portfolio investment to foreign institutional investors (FIIs), proding public sector banks (PSBs) to involve themselves increasingly, both directly and indirectly, in the equity market and fiscal concessions – these efforts have been a heroic failure. In fact, the wise policy would have been to encourage both development banks and the capital market to finance industrial growth. Even public sector banks – which have been highly liquid (the credit-deposit ratio has been hovering around 50 to 52 per cent) – should be encouraged to extend medium-term credit to industries.

Employment holds the key to eradication of poverty but the expansion in employment will not be generated by large and medium industries. One has to look for decentralised growth of a multitude of tiny and small industries in the rural and semi-urban sectors. The Chinese experience is illuminating in this context. To facilitate such broad-based growth we have to develop self-help groups (SHGs), microcredit institutions, and increasingly seek to involve NGOs in the process. It is encouraging that RBI has begun to take some initiatives in this direction.

One of the most retrogressive reforms is the liberalisation of the import of gold. The annual average level of imports of gold works out to a staggering figure of $ 5 billion. Did we raise $ 5.5 billion of forex resources through Resurgent India Bonds (RIBs) to finance the import of gold? Import of gold is destructive of savings because financial savings which could have been channelled to productive purposes, would be diverted to the unproductive investment in gold. Today, in metropolitan and bigger towns there are more jewellery shops than grocery shops. Surely, the WTO did not prescribe the liberalisation of gold imports and this is liberalisation with a vengence. This is a clear case of perversion of priorities in economic reforms, or the ugly face of reforms, a face that has nothing to do even remotely with development.

Finally, efforts to accelerate GDP growth are frustrated, directly or indirectly, by moral pollution. Corruption is so rampant that Mr. N. Vittal, the former Chief Vigilence Commissioner, calls it as "the biggest challenge to the growth of the Society and Nation". Frequent scams in the financial sector, erosion of medical ethics, irregularities in the academic field, and in the health care area – such instances of corruption are eroding economic growth abound. In some states about one-third of the electricity consumption is not "billed" but treated as "transmission and distribution loss" – an euphemism for power theft. The issue of "good governance", which is receiving so much attention recently in development literature, loses much of its relevance in such an environment of pervasive corruption, both financial and moral. There is therefore a need to incorporate what has been tentatively called "the development conscience factor" in development models.

In the ultimate analysis, it is the mindset of policy-makers which really matters. It is hoped that this book would provoke further debate and discussion on the Unaddressed Agenda. Our submission is: let the pace of economic reforms and disinvestment accelerate. Let us liberalise further the policy of import of gold, of import of apples from New Zealand, and of dog food from France. Simultaneously, let us lend some urgency to addressing the problem of productively utilising surplus foodgrains with a view to eliminating hunger and promoting the welfare of the bulk of the population; and to raising the production capabilities of the economy using surplus forex resources. We would have then injected a large dose of development content into economic reforms.

Finally, I must express my grateful thanks to Dr. (Mrs.) Uma Kapila whose persuasive abilities have made possible the early publication of this book. I am indeed deeply indebted to her for the personal interest with which she followed up this project till its completion.

— **N.A. Mujumdar**

I

Macro Perspectives of Growth

1

Building Development Conscience

Going by the discussions in the media on current economic developments in India, the impression may be gained that development simply means liberalisation, privatisation and stabilisation. This shows that our policy-makers are yet to update themselves with the new development thinking and there appears to be some confusion between the means and the ends.

Liberalisation and privatisation have been pursued as ends in themselves rather than as a means to attain more basic objectives of faster and equitable growth, or greater economic stability. These have been pursued even when the consequences have worked against the basic objectives mentioned above.

As Prof. Joseph Stiglitz emphasised: "We must approach development with a more comprehensive framework on awareness of broader objectives and more instruments, a greater sensitivity to the complexity of the development process, a greater sense of humility in the face of the tasks ahead – but also a greater sense of optimism about what the future might bring".[1]

However, not all the elements in the new development thinking are new. Some have resurfaced in mainstream development thinking. In fact, Indian planners in the 1950s were pioneers in emphasising the distributive aspects of national income growth. Blissfully oblivious of these important elements in new development thinking, contemporary Indian policy-makers seem to be busy in building American-style capitalism in India. Some of the ingredients of the new development thinking are:

First, there is no single road to development. The Washington Consensus, on the basis of which economic reforms are largely

1. Proceedings of the Annual World Bank Conference on Development Economics 2000.

modelled, is dated. It would be a mistake to hold up US-style capitalism as the model towards which the world must converge. As Professor Dani Rodrick underlines, "Economic development ultimately derives from a home-grown strategy, not from the world market. Policy-makers in developing countries should avoid fads, put globalisation in perspective, and focus on domestic institution-building. They should have more confidence in themselves and in domestic institution building and place less faith in the global economy and the blueprints emanating thus".[2]

Second, some East-Asian economies have achieved, in recent years, sustained growth with relatively low inequality. They have not followed blindly, as we seem to be doing, the prescriptions of the Washington consensus. The Asian Tigers successfully maintained a high level of macroeconomic stability; but their governments simultaneously played a far more important role than the popular nostrums advised. Thus, new development thinking differs from the old in that distribution of income does matter. The reduction of poverty and inequality assumes importance not only as an end in itself, but also as a means of achieving stronger economic performance.

Third, developmental transformation entails much more than solving technical economic problems with a view to increasing efficiency or facilitating larger resource mobilisation. The focus should be on institutions, such as those that promote competition and good governance in the public and private sectors.

Finally, long-term sustainable growth requires the development of a consensus behind reform policies. Reforms cannot be imported from the outside. Meaningful democratic processes that involve participation and voice, combined with policies that promote equity, can enhance consensus building and a sense of inclusion and even create social capital. These are the broad lines on which Professor Stiglitz has built his arguments.

Indian planners in the 1950s maintained that equity was as important as growth in the development process at a time when the mainstream economists were riding high on the "trickle down"

---

2. *Ibid*

theory of growth. "Enlarge the size of the national cake: its distribution will take care of itself" was the slogan.

Many of these ideas are embedded in the eight learned essays on development planning by the economist Mr. M. Narasimham published between 1988 and 1995, these essays have been included in his book 'Economic Reforms, Development and Finance', published this year.

The steps towards liberalisation are obviously designed to enhance the rate of growth, but, as mentioned earlier, growth alone is not enough. Attention needs to be paid constantly to the social dimensions of growth by expanding social services and building a strong social infrastructure. The priorities would be the eradication of illiteracy and covering the country with primary health care needs and access to safe drinking water.

Or, take the case of equity, "In the words of the South Commission, the declared purpose of development is the eradication of poverty, ignorance and disease. The point has been made that a mere increase in GDP may not be adequate assurance that poverty and other social ills will be eliminated and that too-much reliance should, therefore, not be placed on the 'trickle-down' effect of growth to eliminate poverty". He views elimination of poverty as an aspect of the question of equity.

Again, on the role of the state in economic development, Mr. Narasimham concedes that there is disillusionment with the centralised planning model of the erstwhile Soviet Union. He pleads for decentralised planning as vital to broad-based growth. "The other face of state intervention in developing countries is in respect of directly undertaking investment. In view of the necessity, especially in the earlier stages of economic development, of the provision of social and physical infrastructure would not be attractive in terms of financial return, or where the investment was beyond the resources of the private sector, the state had to assume responsibility for financing investment in these sectors". Contemporary Indian policymakers would do well to ponder over the penetrating analysis of Mr. Narasimham's development process.

Reverting to the question of institution-building, there is one India-specific issue that has not received the attention it deserves.

Contemporary Indian society is plagued by moral pollution and it is time social scientists address the issue. This poses a more dangerous threat to development than, say, environmental pollution, which has attracted good attention.

The rampant corruption includes frequent scams in the financial sector, erosion of medical ethics; irregularity in the academic field, for example, the erratic teaching habits of primary school teachers in village schools, marks-tampering at higher levels of education, and promotions based on considerations other than merit.

Similar irregularities exist in the health-care field – Primary Health Centres may have regular offices in a village and paramedics regularly draw their salaries, but these centres are rarely open for treatment. Finally, there are the fiscal termites – for instance, about one-third of electricity consumption is not 'billed' but treated as 'transmission and distribution losses'. How can a development plan succeed in such an environment?

Thus, there is a need to build "a development conscience" in people. The all-round development of society is achieved through the betterment of the individual and his economic well-being. Social conscience must be inculcated through educational and professional training. There must be sensitivity to the abject poverty, squalor, disease, ignorance and illiteracy surrounding us. The question here is whether to convert the average man into a Baba Amte or an Anna Hazare. The building up of development conscience would go a long way towards improving economic growth and evolving a compassionate society.

The Hindu Business Line, April 6, 2002.

2

Fragility of Growth Base Revealed

The economic reforms, introduced since the crisis year 1991, are an important landmark in the economic history of India. They transformed the closed, centrally planned economy to an open, largely market-driven one.

The reforms included removal of industrial licensing, which abolished restrictions on investment and capacity expansion, de-reservation of industries reserved for the public sector, substantial opening up of foreign direct investment, and trade liberalisation through elimination of quantitative restrictions and reduction in Customs tariffs.

These and related reforms were aimed at promoting faster growth of the economy, aided by improved productivity and efficiency and at making the economy competitive both domestically and globally. In retrospect, can we say that the reforms have produced the intended results?

The main theme of the Reserve Bank of India (RBI) *Report on Currency and Finance 2001-02* is the impact of these policy measures on the economy. The omnibus conclusion of the Report is: "The country has gained significantly from policy reforms." A perceptive reader, however, would find that this is not an unqualified commendation.

Three such insights need to be highlighted. First, for all India's embrace of free-marketry, it has not produced high growth in GDP on a sustainable basis. The euphoria of market enthusiasts that moving over to a market-led economy, would unleash the caged tiger and catapult the economy into a high-growth trajectory, has proved to be ill-founded.

The more recent slowing down of the economy and its attendant problems lend a different perspective to the whole approach to development.

Second, the fragility of the growth base of the economy stands exposed today: GDP growth has slowed down, agricultural growth is stagnating and the domestic saving rate, which is the foundation for larger investment, has actually decelerated.

Economic reforms were indeed 'critical' at the first phase of transforming the economy : having crossed the "critical dose", reforms have to be relegated to a secondary position today. For accelerating growth, what is of utmost importance in the second phase is State activism.

This brings us to the third important conclusion of the report: "India's experience with reforms has reflected the pursuit of an open-ended eclectic and pragmatic approach on questions of economic policy.

The report ends appropriately by quoting the RBI Governor, Dr. Bimal Jalan: "The historical lesson is that most of the successful cases of development are those which have managed to combine the virtues of conflicting paradigms rather than rely exclusively on a single-set of preordained theoretically right policies".

The boldness of the RBI experts in advocating the formula of public-private sector mix, at a time when the theology of marketing seems to have swayed the present-day policy-makers, need to be acclaimed. The exaggerated importance given to the privatisation of petroleum companies – HPCL and BPCL – as if privatisation is the panacea for the ills of the economy is illustrative of the privatisation philosophy dominating the present day policy-makers. This exuberance needed to be moderated.

The trend in GDP growth in more recent years is of serious concern. The initial euphoria of reforms producing a 6 per cent growth on a continuing basis has practically evaporated. It is not merely a question of a drought year of 2002-03 producing a growth of 4.4 per cent.

During the six years from 1997-98 to 2002-03, as many as three years recorded a growth rate of only 4.5 per cent. In respect of agriculture, the trend rate of growth stagnated at 2.5 per cent during the ten-year period, 1992-93 to 2002-03. Against this backdrop, how does one hope to attain the targets of 8 per cent growth in GDP and some 4 per cent of agricultural growth, envisaged in the Tenth Plan?

Again, gross domestic savings, which provide the basis for larger investment, actually declined from 24.4 per cent of GDP during the period, 1994-95 to 1996-97, to 23.5 per cent of GDP in the period 1997-98 to 2001-02. The Tenth Plan expects to raise the saving rate to 26.8 per cent of GDP. It is time those who delude themselves that the opening up of the economy would automatically result in acceleration of growth realised that the growth base itself has been eroded. Some corrective measures need to be introduced. The most conspicuous example is agriculture, in a way the victim of reforms.

This sector was neglected: public investment in the sector declined, net addition to irrigated area decelerated, flow of institutional credit suffered a set back. In fact, the rural credit delivery system is in a moribund state today. The immediate need is, therefore, not so much for reforms as for State activism in terms of larger public investment, large incremental areas of irrigation, extension, micro watershed development programmes and so on.

Two misconceptions about reforms contributing to agricultural growth need to be cleared. First, the report seems elated about the setting up of the commodity exchanges for trading in futures and options in agricultural commodities. It is naive to believe that these exchanges, even when they function effectively, would bring about improvement in the prices received by the average farmer.

The havoc that private trade played in foodgrains and cotton trade in the not-too-distant past is too well-known to need repetition: artificially depressing farm prices in the immediate post-harvest period and raising them to high levels in the lean period. It is in this context that the Food Corporation of India (FCI) emerged as a counterbalancing force.

Now, the second misconception. To quote the Report again: "A factor contributing to the below potential performance of agriculture is the failure to sufficiently diversify the cropping pattern. The minimum support price (MSP) policy has distorted the relative prices between rice and wheat on the one hand, and other food and non-food crops, on the other, giving rise to a distorted cropping pattern.

"...There is a need to re-examine the price support mechanism to eliminate the distortion of agricultural product composition in line with diversification of the consumption basket of a representative

Indian household: There has been some acceleration in the growth of high value-added agricultural products such as milk, fruits and vegetables, poultry, meat and fisheries during the 1990." Do RBI experts believe that the accumulation of rice and wheat of more than 40 million tonnes with the FCI is due to lack of demand for foodgrains?

Elsewhere in the Report it is stated: "The per capita availability has remained below the historic peak attained in 1991". We need larger quantities of foodgrains to meet the minimum needs of nutrition of the entire population.

Higher agricultural growth should also come from improvement in the average yields of foodgrains. We may have a second look at MSP policy for other reasons but not for because we have surplus foodgrains. No doubt, the food basket of the middle-class has become diversified with high-value foods such as milk and meat. But the fact remains that the food basket of the poor, who constitute about one-fourth of the population, continues to remain either half empty or empty altogether.

On the imperative need to raise the savings rate, the critical factor is to raise the household sector's savings, which constitute the bulk of financial savings. Reforms borrowed from the kitty of IMF-World Bank theology, have proved counter-productive.

In an overzealous attempt to develop the capital market, several artificial props were provided. Fiscal concessions were extended to investment in equity and, not to say, bank deposits, which in India constitute a dominant segment of household sector's savings.

Despite these props, the capital market is in a moribund state today : resources raised through the primary issues had reached a peak of Rs. 17,414 crore in 1994-95; the average level of resources raised during the last three years works out to Rs. 7,000 crore. The low interest rate regime has also given a serious blow to household savings.

The recent upheaval of the UTI was also a major shock to savers in the household sector. The whole range of the so-called reforms designed to develop the capital market needs to be re-examined.

If in the Indian milieu bank deposits are an appropriate instrument for mobilising household sector's savings, why scuttle them by mindless policies? They should be given a level-playing field with investments in equity. Interest rate policies need to be re-examined in this light.

By producing such a highly analytical report on the impact of economic reforms on the growth of the economy, RBI experts have achieved two major things. They have shaken the eulogists of reforms out of their self-induced stupor.

Economic reforms were indeed necessary and welcome: but, by themselves, they have not produced any Schumpeterean heroes. There are such heroes in the software and IT industry, but their emergence has nothing to do with reforms.

In fact, reforms have rendered the growth base rather fragile. If growth is to be accelerated in the coming years, the State must step in again. The second generation of reforms thus become, not critical, but marginal.

The Planning Commission waxes eloquent on the economy's post-reform performance. "The Tenth Plan (2002-07) has been prepared against a backdrop of high expectations arising from some aspects of the recent performance. GDP growth in the post-reform period has improved from an average about 5.7 per cent in the 1980s to an average of about 6.1 per cent in the Eight and Ninth Plan periods, making India one of the ten fastest growing countries in the world".

The fragility of the growth base witnessed in more recent years should make the Planning Commission sit up and re-think strategies to accelerate growth.

The Hindu Business Line, April 29, 2003

3

Policy Makers vs Econometricians

The deceleration of the economic growth seems to be persisting. GDP growth rate declined from 6.6 per cent in 1998-99 to 6.4 per cent in 1999-2000, and further down to 5.2 per cent in 2000-01. The growth rate during the first half of 2001-02 at 5.3 per cent is distinctly lower than the 6.2 per cent recorded during the corresponding previous period.

The Reserve Bank of India's team of experts deserves to be commended for addressing this issue of slowdown, now a global phenomenon. 'Revitalising Growth' is the theme of the RBI's Report on Currency and Finance for 2000-01. Does it provide any readymade policy inputs? It is legitimate to ask this question because the RBI Deputy Governor, Dr. Y.V. Reddy, makes the following statement in his Foreword: "As in the past, the approach is one of policy-oriented research and empirical verification so that public opinion is suitably empowered with information and specialised assessment. In fact, the Report exposes the great divide between the policy-maker, whose feet are firmly on the ground and the econometrician who lives in a world of abstract models.

The econometrician is known to be "massaging" the data, cleaning them of peaks and troughs, so that he reaches the conclusions he set out to reach in the beginning. The divide is, perhaps, all for the good, otherwise, if the policy-maker accepts all the recommendations of the econometrician as gospel truth, there is the danger of the economy running into rough weather!

One may begin with the interesting insights provided by the penetrating analysis of the Report. An important finding is that the current phase of slow down represents "a loss of spread rather than a halt in growth. Cyclical patterns in activity are detected but these are of limited duration and impact. The Indian economy is characterised by stable and converging cycles which could be modulated with counter cyclical policies. The impulses for growth can be generated and nurtured primarily by releasing the structural constraints which can shift the potential growth frontiers upwards"

The RBI experts have avoided the temptation to explain the slowdown in terms of business cycles, as in the case of some developed economies. It must be added that the slowdown is a deceleration in growth and not a slump. Even the pessimistic forecast of growth for 2001-02 places the growth rate at around 5 per cent – way above the so-called Hindu rate of growth. 'Revitalising Growth', as Dr. Reddy puts it, is perhaps, a more appropriate description of the theme. If the target 8 per cent growth is to be sustained in the Tenth Five-Year Plan (2002-07), as envisaged by the Draft Approach Paper, how does one go about it? It is here that the "spread of growth" concept assumes significance. Spread could be sectoral or regional. If GDP is to grow at 8 per cent, the agricultural sector has to grow at some 4 per cent. This is a tautology but policy-makers ignored this aspect in the 1990s when the average annual growth of agriculture decelerated from 5.2 per cent in the 1980s to 2.6 per cent. The flow of credit to agriculture shrank and so on.

Again, the banking sector was caught napping when the new revolution in the information technology took place. Only in the late 1990s did the RBI and banks wake up to assist the IT sector. In terms of regional spread, some regions have the potential to grow faster than others, given the injection of some quantum of capital. The Report has placed firmly on the development agenda the requirement that all policies, including monetary and credit policies, should focus on the "spread" aspect of growth.

Equally interesting is the insight provided by the Report on the capital market, which comes as a refreshing change from the obsessive preoccupation of the present-day policy-makers with the development of the capital market. The report poses the question: "Which system – capital market-based or financial intermediation – is more efficient in the long run in allocating financial resources?"

The two competing systems appear to be converging in recent years. In Japan and Germany – economies where banks play a crucial role – capital markets are becoming increasingly important. On the other hand, in the US, banks are increasingly required to play a greater role in corporate finance. The Report, therefore, recommends a suitable mix of the two: "Thus, the co-existence of both the systems is socially desirable not only because it encourages competition but also because it reduces transaction costs within the financial system and helps improve resource allocation within the economy". India's policy-makers would do well to heed this advice because, with so many artificial props given to boost the capital market and the discrimination against commercial and development banks, the capital market has failed to develop.

Among the disturbing recommendations of the report, the two relating to inflation and savings need to be highlighted. During this financial year so far, inflation declined sharply to 1.32 per cent (week ended January 19). Then, is this deflation responsible for the slowdown? The Report asserts that it is so. Threshold inflation – that is, growth maximising inflation rate – is estimated at 5 per cent. There are potential output losses involved in further disinflation. Sacrifice ratio estimates suggest that in a low inflation environment, a one percentage point reduction in inflation leads to a decline in output by two percentage point below the potential". This assertion is repeated elsewhere in the Report also. This recommendation is bound to shock many balanced policy-makers. Conventional wisdom based on cross-country empirical experience has always maintained that a moderate inflation is good for a developing economy. The objective, therefore, should be to aim at not zero inflation but, say, 1 or 2 per cent inflation. Beyond that level, inflation creates distortions in income distribution and affects employment adversely. Similarly, in the 1970s, there were years when the inflation was moderate, say, below 2 per cent and yet, growth was not sacrificed. In any case, this conclusion of the report needs a second look. Is infirmity or massaging of data responsible for the emergence of such an unrealistic conclusion?

The Report's profound observations on savings are equally perplexing to conventional analysts. "Other things remaining the same, a one per cent increase each in income and intermediation ratio (secondary issues to primary issues ratio, as used in flow of funds accounts), would increase the aggregate saving rate by 6.6 percentage points and 3.4 percentage points, respectively. The interest rate, that is, real deposit rate has a lesser but positive impact on gross savings rate, implying that as much as 12 per cent points change in the real interest rate is required to increase aggregate savings by one percentage point. The results indicate that the dynamic response of the private saving rate to per capita income (per capita disposable income in the relevant scale variable in studying private saving behaviour) works out to 7.8".

An increase of 12 per cent in real interest rate to achieve one per cent rise in aggregate saving rate? Bewildering. Are household sectors's financial savings, that account for the bulk of aggregate financial savings in the economy, interest-sensitive? Or is there a threshold beyond which they become interest-sensitive? These questions are critical in the Indian context because historically, banks have attracted deposits of the household sector, not withstanding infirmities such as relatively lower interest rates, and taxability of interest income, and tax deduction at source. In any case, to those familiar with the saving behaviour of the household sector, a 12 per cent real increase looks astronomical. Similarly, what is the economic meaning of the intermediation ratio in the Indian capital market? These issues need to be thoroughly re-examined before arriving at such a startling conclusion.

The report is euphoric that capital flows have begun to play a significant role in India's growth dynamics. Evidence of strong complementarity with domestic investment suggests that capital flows brighten the overall investment climate and stimulate domestic investment even when a part of the capital flows actually gets absorbed in the form of accretion to reserves. What about the utilisation of reserves? The report is silent on this aspect, perhaps, because the model does not capture this dimension. If we spend $7 billion annually on the import of gold, how does accretion of reserves help growth? Gold imports neither enhance productive capacity of the economy nor its export capability. But this aspect of appropriate utilisation of reserves does not interest model builders.

Then there are more mundane issues. The report refers to the huge foodgrains stocks with the public sector, aggregating to 59.1 million tonnes at the end of November 2001. That there is enormous scope for undertaking watershed development programmes is too well-known. How about using a part of these surplus foodgrains to facilitate the undertaking of such programmes on a massive scale?

This would go some way towards revitalising growth, in terms of more employment, higher rural incomes, food security and reduction of poverty. But such mundane matters, perhaps, can not be captured by elegant econometric models.

On the whole, the policy-maker is bound to benefit by the interesting insights provided by the report into the functioning of the economy. At the same time, there is some merit in the Indian policy-maker maintaining some distance from the econometrician. Policy-making remains an art, it cannot be replaced by software.

The Hindu Business Line, February 5, 2002.

4

Upgrading Productive Capabilities

Does the Budget lack a strategy, if not a grand design, for accelerating the growth of the economy? The answer is that the Budget has an underlying strategy: the Finance Minister could have improved the presentability of the Budget by spelling out the strategy, instead of leaving it to be discovered by perceptive observers. The clue to the strategy is provided by the following paragraph towards the end of the Budget speech: "This Budget is devoted to development. This is a Budget to further promote partnership with the States for a better tomorrow for the people of India." This statement cannot be dismissed as the usual Budget rhetoric because there are concrete measures embodied in the Budget to achieve the objectives.

In fact, the Finance Minister has addressed the larger issues of the economy beyond the corporate sector with which the media, particularly the visual media, seems obsessed. No wonder the corporate sector felt initially disappointed, with the Bombay Stock Exchange Sensex declining sharply by 143 points or by 4 per cent to 3,562 on the Budget day. This irrational depression was corrected the very next day when the Sensex rose 136 points to 3,679.

In any case, the stock market has since long ceased to be the barometer of business confidence and, hence, one must not read too much into these irrational movements. Three characteristic features of the Budget need to be highlighted.

First, the Budget seeks to spread the growth impulses in different segments of the economy. Second, in India, the business of development is a cooperative enterprise between the Centre and the states and this Budget has taken initiatives to goad the states, as it were, to play their role in the development process. Third, the strategy is aimed at upgrading the growth capability of the economy in the medium term and, hence, it may not immediately translate itself into accelerated growth.

It may be recalled at this stage that the RBI's recent Report On Currency and Finance had come to the conclusion that the current slowdown of the economy represents "a loss of spread rather than a halt in growth. Cyclical patterns in activity are detected but these are of limited duration and impact... The impulses for growth can be generated and nurtured primarily by releasing the structural constraints which can shift the potential growth frontiers upwards."

Perhaps taking a cue from this diagnosis, the Finance Minister has focussed on the 'spread' aspect of growth. This has two dimensions: sectoral and regional. Taking the first dimension: if the economy has to grow at, say, 7 to 8 per cent per annum, the farm sector has to grow necessarily by 4 per cent. This is a tautology but the policy-makers ignored this in the 1990s when the average annual growth of agriculture fell sharply from 5.2 per cent in the 1980s to 2.6 per cent. The measures embodied in the Budget to promote agricultural growth, in particular, and rural development, in general, have to be judged against this background.

The credit for according a pre-eminent position to agricultural and rural development on the development agenda must go to the Finance Minister, who has characterised this phase of agricultural diversification and food processing as the Third Revolution, following the Green and White Revolutions. The allocation for the accelerated irrigation benefit programme (AIBP) has been stepped up from Rs. 2,000 crore this year to Rs. 2,800 crore in 2002-03. This should help the states accelerate the completion of unfinished major and medium irrigation projects and also to undertake reforms by revising user charges and setting up water-users' associations.

Similarly, the allocation for rural infrastructural development fund (RIDF VIII) has been increased from Rs. 5,000 crore to Rs. 5,500 crore, while the rate of interest for these funds has been reduced from 10.5 per cent to 8.5 per cent. Kisan Credit Cards introduced in 1998-99 have made considerable progress, the total number reaching 2.07 crore. This has enhanced the reach of farmers to rural credit. In micro credit, a good beginning has been made with the number of self-help groups (SHGs) rising to some 3.5 lakh covering some 20 lakh families. Then there are programmes for rural roads and housing, and employment, all of which would lead to generation of higher rural incomes.

Yet another sector which the Budget seeks to activate is the small-scale industries (SSI). With trade liberalisation complete, the SSI sector is now subject to increasing competition and, hence, a new approach is needed to revitalise the sector. The Credit Guarantee Scheme and the Credit Linked Capital Subsidy Scheme for Technological Upgradation have already facilitated larger flow of credit to this sector. Encouraged by the success of the Kisan Credit Cards, Public Sector Banks have now decided to introduce a scheme called Laghu Udyami Credit Card (LUCC) scheme for providing simplified and borrower-friendly credit facilities to small businessmen, retail traders, artisians and micro entrepreneurs, and professionals.

The Chinese experience in this context is relevant. During two decades of sustained growth of some 10 per cent per annum, China was able to reduce poverty to 3 per cent of the population. To a considerable extent, this is attributed to the explosion of non-farm employment in the rural sector and microcredit institutions supported the growth of micro businesses. This experience is worthy of emulation.

There is an analytical basis for this approach of the Budget to spread growth. Following received wisdom, many experts have been arguing that the current slowdown in the economy is due to demand recession and the remedy lies in reducing taxes – both individual and corporate – to boost aggregate disposable income. Unfortunately, this is not applicable to the Indian situation because the total number of tax payers is only 2.5 crores. Reduction of taxes in this situation would not achieve anything, except loss of revenue.

The alternative route adopted by the Budget is to boost growth in sectors other than industry, which refuse to grow at more than 3 to 4 per cent. If the aggregate income stream swells as a result of spread of growth, the objective of accelerating the overall growth of the economy would be achieved.

In respect of the second characteristic feature, implementation of several development programmes depends on states' response. For instance, there is ample money available under the integrated rural development fund (IRDF) scheme, but its utilisation is dismally low at some 30 per cent. Many States are not enthusiastic about utilising these funds, partly because it involves a lot of homework in terms of preparation of projects, monitoring, and so on.

Similarly, there is a complaint that some states have not made full use of free foodgrains the Centre sought to provide for the purpose of food-for-work programmes. It is in this context that the carrots provided in the Budget to induce states to undertake some project or to introduce fiscal reforms become relevant.

On food management, the Centre's proposal to involve states in terms of decentralised procurement has not been acceptable. The attempts by the Centre to reduce the size of the huge mountain of foodgrains of 60 million tonnes have not been successful. Allocation of some 30 lakh tonnes to states for relief works and another 30 lakh tonnes for open market operations – it is only allocation and not utilisation – does not mean much.

Had the Finance Minister provided, say, some 10 million tonnes of foodgrains, free of cost, to states for use in the micro watershed development schemes on a massive scale, perhaps, the medium-term gains to farmers involved and also to the economy, as a whole, would far outweigh the costs of these foodgrains.

One wishes that the Finance Minister had taken such a bold step, without waiting for the Report of the High Level committee on Long Term Grain Policy. Such a move would fall into the category of measures designed to upgrade the productive capability of the economy.

The Finance Minister deserves to be congratulated on his bold action of withdrawing the tax exemption granted to dividend income. In India, household sector is the major contributor to the total financial savings and bank deposits account for the bulk of the household sectors financial savings. Exemption of dividend income from personal tax, thus, discriminated against bank deposits. There was no economic rationale for this measure. It is good that this distortion has been corrected now.

In the Indian context, encouraging savings in the form of bank deposits is as important as encouraging investment in the capital market. It is also necessary to add that the reduction, by 50 basis points, in the interest rate on small-savings such as National Savings Certificates, Public Provident Fund, is a retrograde step.

The arithmetic of those experts who have argued that since inflation has declined to 1.1 per cent, there is a case for reduction of the interest rate, is flawed. The 1.1 per cent inflation refers to a point-to-point basis.

Inflation on the basis of 52-week average remains high at 4.7 per cent. Inflation expectations are also high at 5 per cent and, hence, there was no case for reduction in interest on small savings.

If, today, India can boast of a high saving rate of 25 per cent of GDP, the credit for raising the savings rate goes to commercial banks and small savings. Hence, any measure which results in the erosion of the savings habit should be shunned.

The Hindu Business Line, March 12, 2002.

5

Foodgrains Surplus, Forex Reserves

Problem of Plenty or Plus Point?

Indian planners and bureaucrats are adept at managing a shortage economy. When it comes to 'affluence' in some segments of the economy, however, the policy-makers seem ill-equipped to use the 'surpluses' to accelerate the growth of the economy or better realise the end-objectives of development. This is the broad conclusion that any perceptive reader of the RBI Annual Report for 2001-02 would arrive at.

The analysis of the recent developments in the economy clearly shows that the prospects for growth in 2002-03 are marred by the ominous drought : 19 out of 36 meteorological sub-divisions received deficient or scanty rainfall, compared to only seven sub-divisions the previous year.

This necessitated the downward revision of projected GDP growth from 6 per cent to 6.5 per cent to around 5 per cent. In fact, we do not seem to appreciate that such a widespread drought would have, in normal times, proved disastrous for the economy, bringing in its wake nominal or nil growth, high inflation and large-scale starvation.

Three factors have saved us from such a possible calamity. First, the economy has inherited from previous years an embarrassingly large stock of foodgrains — some 63 million tonnes at end-June 2002.

Second, the country's foreign exchange reserves have reached a new peak of some \$ 60 billion, equivalent to some 15 months of imports. The country can thus freely import any food item, including edible oils, to compensate for domestic scarcity.

Third, inflation is subdued. Inflation, as measured by the wholesale prices on a year-on-year basis, declined to 2.7 per cent on August 3, 2002, from 5.5 per cent a year ago.

Historically, the refrain of Indian planners has been that the availability of foodgrains and foreign exchange are the main constraints to economic growth. Now that these constraints have been removed, at least for the last couple of years, why is India still unable to join the league of high growth economies such as the Asian Tigers, or even China?

One is disappointed that the RBI *pundits* have not even attempted to explore the possibilities of accelerating growth with the use of foodgrains and foreign exchange surpluses.

Part of the explanation for the relatively slower growth of the economy is that, post-1990, when we changed over to the so-called market-led economy, courting the corporate elite has become an objective of macroeconomic policy. The corporate sector wants a low interest rate regime and the interest rate structure has been changed accordingly.

Today, an MNC or a high-rated corporate entity can raise funds from banks at 8 or 9 per cent, whereas a small farmer has to pay minimum interest rate of 12 per cent. The corporate sector wants the capital market to be developed and the Government has gone out of its way to promote the capital market: fiscal concessions for investment in equity; throwing open portfolio investment to foreign institutional investors; persuading Public Sector Banks to increasingly involve themselves, directly and indirectly, in the capital market; and so on.

It does not matter if sectors such as agriculture or small industries do not have access to the capital market. And it is a different matter that all these heroic efforts have failed. For instance, the total resources mobilised from the primary market added up to just Rs. 7,111 crore in 2001-02. In sharp contrast, the resources raised through private placements soared to nearly Rs. 65,000 crore.

Dr. S.S. Tarapore, former Deputy Governor, RBI, sums up the situation in the following words: "The problem with the Indian system is that entrepreneurs have got habituated to unsustainable large borrowings with minimal-owned funds. Any successful entrepreneur must realise that borrowing should only be the icing on the cake and internal generation should form the predominant element. Thus, the question which needs to be posed is not how to stimulate the flow of funds from intermediaries to industry but how industry can become self-financing. Making the interest rate too attractive and credit too easy to obtain is a sure path to disaster".

A corollary of this focus on the corporate sector or large and medium industries was the neglect of agriculture, small industries and microenterprises. Public investment in agriculture, particularly irrigation, declined. And the flow of credit to the rural sector decelerated; in fact, the rural credit delivery system became moribund.

The policy-makers must realise that despite industrial expansion and export growth, agriculture will remain the main source of livelihood for the bulk of the population. Over the years, though the share of agriculture in national income, or GDP, has declined substantially from 50 per cent to only 25 per cent, dependence on agriculture has declined only marginally. It is still the means of livelihood of as many as 60 per cent of the population. Hence, broad-based rural development should be at the centre of the overall development strategy.

It is refreshing to note that the RBI Annual report recognises the importance of agricultural development, when it says: "Variability in agricultural production has emerged as a cause for serious concern.... There is an urgent need to increase public investment in irrigation and water management, given the high correlation between the growth of area under high yielding varieties of seeds and gross irrigated area,". The Report adds: "Moreover, investment needs to be directed towards watershed development in view of its salutary environmental implications."

One wishes that the RBI experts could have gone further here, instead of being content with making such a general statement. Using surplus foodgrains to promote rural development and welfare become relevant here. The success of this approach lies in linking the use of surplus foodgrains to productive activities.

The most conspicuous programme that comes to mind is the micro-watershed in development programme, which can be undertaken on a massive scale throughout the country. The bulk of the cost of such programmes would be accounted for by wages that can be paid in kind, namely foodgrains.

The technology involved is simple, and village Panchayats can implement these schemes. Thus, using surplus foodgrains, it is possible to create additional employment and income for the rural poor, while at the same time creating large overload capital. Insurance against drought is another aspect of the gain to the economy.

Another lesson India can learn about its growth pattern is from the Chinese experience. China was able to reduce rural poverty to only 6 per cent of the population in a matter of two decades. This was, in large part, due to the fact that there was an explosion in non-farm employment. Rural industry grew sizably, employing 25 per cent of the rural labour force. Township and Village Enterprises (TVE) expanded rapidly, contributing 40 per cent to the total industrial output. Access to subsidised credit was an important factors that facilitated such rapid growth.

The point to drive home is that financial and credit policies should be so shaped as to facilitate the growth and expansion of such microenterprises. Although the annual report makes a passing reference to microcredit institutions, there is no specific agenda for the promotion of microcredit institutions. It is easier to wax eloquent on implementing financial sector reforms, by replicating the models embodied in the IMF, World Bank prescriptions or BIS norms. It is more difficult to evolve our own model of a network of microcredit institutions linked to NGOs and self-help groups (SHGs).

Management of the country's foreign exchange reserves is an art. The level of reserves should be adequate to inspire confidence but not excessive. Maintaining excess reserves is wasteful, especially when the interest rates in developed countries such as the US or the UK are at their lowest. In other words, yields on reserves have declined to their lowest levels. The present level of our reserves — $ 60 billion — is indeed excessive, considering that it is equivalent to 15 months imports.

Generally, reserves equivalent to some six months of imports is regarded as reasonable. Our efforts should, therefore, be directed towards using part of the reserves for financing imports of capital or intermediate goods which would boost our domestic production capacity. These imports may be used to develop infrastructure like power or transport. Thus, using foodgrains surplus for productive activities and forex reserves to import capital goods would go some way to upgrade the production capability of the economy. It may not result in accelerating GDP growth immediately, but its impact on GDP growth would be certainly felt in the medium term.

The RBI report should have also emphasised the primordiality of drought-relief during this year. What purpose will the mountain of surplus foodgrains serve if they cannot be used immediately to feed the unemployed and the poor? What is, after all, the end objective of development? Reduction of poverty, unemployment and starvation. In fact, the stocks with the Food Corporation of India (FCI) should be available on tap to all the states affected by drought.

For now, the Government should ignore the fiscal deficit target and the RBI its monetary target. In any case, the use of foodgrains on the lines discussed here will not generate inflationary pressures. Such a strategy of using surplus foodgrains and foreign exchange resources would place the economy on an optimum growth trajectory.

The Hindu Business Line, October 3, 2002.

6

Words of Wisdom

The *Economic Survey 2002-03* is a massive document of 246 pages and the appended statistical statements run to another 115 pages. The impact of such a scholarly document is muffled mainly because of three reasons. First, the *Survey* is released a day before the presentation of the Budget and the common man is more directly concerned with the dust and din raised by the Budget. To him, the *Survey* remains an academic document.

Second, over the years, the *Survey* has acquired the characteristics of a Ph.D thesis – prolix and discursive. This lack of focus has meant that its policy recommendations are lost in the maze of facts and figures. If a discerning policymaker wades through the labyrinthine intricacies of data and detailed discussions, he is bound to discover words of wisdom, which can serve as important policy inputs. And, third, the canvas of the *Survey* is not constrained by the arithmetic of a single year's Budget exercise. Its coverage extends to wider policy issues which continue to be relevant even after the dust raised by the Budget settles down.

The *Survey's* impact on Budget-specific issues is, therefore, somewhat limited. To influence future policy formulation more effectively, it would be useful if the *Survey* provided a separate chapter, say, an Executive Summary, listing its main recommendations which have the potential of serving as policy inputs.

The following issues could be taken up for discussion: crowding-out effects of fiscal deficit; currency backing; output-money-price relationship; surplus foodgrains and food subsidies; and the medium-term outlook for growth. That the mounting fiscal deficit is intrinsically harmful has been repeated *ad nauseam*.

For the Centre, fiscal deficit as a proportion of GDP has gone up from 4.1 per cent in 1996-97 to 5.9 per cent in 2001-02. And the combined deficit of both the Centre and States has risen from 9.5 per cent in 1999-2000 to 10 per cent in 2001-02.

The *Survey* has added a new dimension to this worry by warning that financing of such large deficits is likely to crowd out private investment: "Given the indices of growth recovery already visible, without fiscal consolidation there is a risk that the pre-emption of resources by the government will crowd out the nascent recovery in private investment." Take the case of commercial banks. While the statutory liquidity ratio (SLR) prescribes that banks invest 25 per cent of their deposits in government securities, the actual investment-deposit ratio was a high 42 per cent in February 2003. In other words, such large banking sector resources, far in excess of the prescribed levels, are being diverted away from productive sectors of the economy to the Government.

Perhaps, even such diversion could be justified if the resources are utilised for capital expenditure or investment. Unfortunately, the resources now go merely to supporting government consumption. For years now, the Centre has been running up huge deficits on its current revenue account.

The RBI's flawed public debt management policy is partly to blame for this. There was time when the yield on government securities (G-Secs) was raised to 14 per cent and Public Sector Banks preferred to park much of their funds in these securities rather than lend to productive sectors of the economy. Fortunately, the yields on G-Secs have now fallen considerably and there is little incentive for banks to invest substantial resources in them. But Public Sector Banks have become accustomed to exercising the "soft option" of investing in G-Secs.

To defer them from doing so, it is necessary to prescribe a ceiling; for instance, banks should not be allowed to invest more than, say, 30 per cent of their deposits in G-Secs at any point of time. Only such a drastic measure would 'normalise' the operations of banks, which are now practically underwriting the public borrowing programme of the Central Government.

On the conventional "currency backing" concept, the *Survey* provides some interesting insights: "The strengthening of the balance of payments has impacted on the monetary sector, with net foreign exchange assets (NFA) of the RBI emerging as an important source of reserve money. From 9.1 per cent as at end-March 1991, the share of net foreign assets in reserve money, which had reached 78.1 per cent by end of 2001-02, became 100.7 per cent on January 24, 2003, which is close to a currency boards situation."

The reference here is to the currency boards in the colonial era, when 100 per cent "backing" of domestic currency – either by gold or pound sterling – expansion was required. Whatever may have been the virtues or vices of such currency board prescriptions, the *Survey* should have spelt out the contemporary policy implications of money supply expansion caused largely by accretion to foreign exchange reserves.

In such a situation, domestic money supply does not faithfully reflect the state of aggregate demand. It is necessary to drive home this point, especially to those who cry wolf about the large budget deficit and the consequent danger of the emerging inflation.

In fact, there is a deeper issue for monetarists to ponder over. The more recent trends seem to pose the question: has the conventional output-money-prices relationship broken down?

During the past three years, while GDP growth averaged 4.8 per cent, money supply expansion continued to be high at around 15.5 per cent. And yet, inflation remained a low 3.6 per cent per annum. This is especially impressive because, as the *Survey* reminds us, "drought in 17 States this year after 14 years of normal or near normal rainfall (last drought was in 1987) raised apprehension of high inflation in 2002-03."

Inflation, even on a 52-week-average basis, remained low at 2.6 per cent in 2002-03. One may by all means condemn high budgetary deficits, but it would be analytically flawed to argue that such deficits would automatically lead to high inflation. The "quality" of money supply expansion, if one may use such an expression, is relevant in this context.

Money supply expansion caused primarily by the accretion in forex reserves is quite different from the expansion caused largely by domestic factors. The policy responses in the two situations would be, or at least should be, different. Moreover, the embarrassingly high 48.2 million tonnes of foodgrain stocks and forex reserves of

$75 billion provide enough elbow room to control inflation, if inflationary forces do threaten to emerge.

Enough has been said about the mountain of foodgrain stocks which, at one point had crossed 60 million tonnes. There is no use now blaming the minimum support price (MSP) system for this chaotic situation. For the past couple of years, the stocks with the Food Corporation of India (FCI), have been way above the prescribed buffer stock norm of 16.8 million tonnes. The *Survey* offers a more pragmatic solution: "Strong corrective steps aligning the minimum support prices with the cost of production of foodgrains are called for. Perhaps, the only solution we have at hand is to freeze the current MSP until such time it becomes equal to the cost, or until annual procurement settles down to earlier levels of 24-30 million tonnes."

Even the efforts of the Government to utilise surplus foodgrains under various welfare schemes, such as Annapurna, earthquake relief, food for work, mid-day meal, and so on, have been rather half-hearted. No doubt, the off-take under nine such schemes jumped from 32 lakh tonnes in 2000-01 to 71 lakh tonnes in 2001-02, but in 2002-03, the off-take was a 75 lakh tonnes. Given, particularly, the drought situation, there is no reason why the off-take should not have shown a quantum jump in 2002-03.

The *Survey* justifies an element of food subsidy: "The merits of the MSP in achieving the objective of food security is established. So is the general consensus that some food subsidy is absolutely essential for providing income support to the country's poor and vulnerable. Apart from providing subsidised foodgrains to the below poverty line (BPL) population (over 30 crore) a most significant and innovative measure to address abject poverty is the Antyodaya Anna Yojana which enables a section of the poorest (about six crore) to obtain 35 kg of foodgrains per month at the low price of Rs. 2 per kg for wheat and the Rs. 3 per kg for rice." It is perhaps the success of this scheme which promoted the Finance Minister to announce that the Antyodaya scheme would be expanded to cover an additional 50 lakh families, raising the total coverage to more than a quarter of all BPL families during 2003-04.

The *Survey* provides interesting insights into the medium-term outlook for growth. In the first year (2002-03) of the Tenth Plan

(2002-07), which envisages an average annual GDP growth of 8 per cent, a GDP growth of 4.4 per cent is way below the target. But it should be recognised that the overall GDP growth was depressed because of a decline in agricultural sector growth by 3.1 per cent.

In contrast, there was an across-the-board improvement in the growth of both industry and services, from 3.3 per cent to 6.1 per cent and from 6.8 per cent to 7.1 per cent, respectively. This recovery in non-agricultural sectors "was accompanied by continued macroeconomic stability in terms of low inflation, orderly currency market conditions and comfortable reserves."

Superimposed on these salutary developments is the buoyancy in exports, which in dollar terms were growing at 20.4 per cent during April-December 2002. The exports surge "has occurred in spite of the sluggish pace of global economic recovery, and the slight appreciation of the rupee *vis-à-vis* the dollar and has contributed to domestic industrial growth." The current account of the Balance of Payments recorded a surplus for the first time in 23 years, of 0.3 per cent of GDP in 2001-02. The buoyant exports and net invisible inflows are likely to results in a surplus on current account for the second year in succession. On the whole, the *Survey* seems to conclude that despite the setback to overall GDP growth in the first year of the Tenth Plan, "international evidence as well as India's own experience demonstrates that the target (of 8 per cent growth) in indeed feasible."

It would be appropriate to conclude with the following quote from the *Survey*: "Nevertheless, there is an imperative need to address the three issues of infrastructure, regulatory and tax reform, and fiscal consolidation to establish the foundation of robust growth on a sustainable basis."

The Hindu Business Line, March 28, 2003

7

The Development Conscience Factor

Contemporary society seems to be afflicted by moral pollution which adversely affects economic development in a variety of ways and it is high time that social scientists address this issue. This sort of pollution poses a far more dangerous threat to development, than, say, environmental pollution which has attracted a good deal of attention both nationally and internationally. This moral pollution afflicts, though in different ways, developed countries like the US, emerging market economies like India and also transition economics like Russia. A preliminary analysis of this feature of contemporary society suggests that there is an imperative need to incorporate what has been tentatively called the "development conscience factor" in development models – tentatively because a more expressive phrase is not readily available. The proposal to build the development conscience factor – a concept which is – religious – is designed to tackle the moral pollution. Accelerating economic growth is undoubtedly a pre-requisite for reducing poverty, eliminating illiteracy and disease among the bulk of the population; but this goal is not exclusive of the broader objective of evolving an egalitarian, just, humane and compassionate society. Improving the quality of life of the bulk of the population, which is the end-objective of all development endeavours could be rendered possible only in the environs of such a society. In the ultimate analysis, therefore, we should have a clear vision of what sort of society we should seek to evolve, alongside our efforts to accelerate economic growth. In the absence of such a vision, we may end up merely producing a caricature of growth. Viewed from this broader perspective, economic development endeavour will not remain the exclusive preserve of economic model builders, but would become a cooperative endeavour of social scientists like economists, sociologists, philosophers and educationists. Development conscience thus emerges as the fifth factor of production, in addition to the four enumerated in classical economic literature.

In the case of India, efforts to accelerate the GDP growth are frustrated, directly or indirectly, by moral pollution Corruption is so rampant that Mr. N. Vittal, the former Chief Vigilance Commissioner calls it as the "biggest challenge to the growth of the society and nation." This is not confined to public sector but is all pervasive. There are frequent scams in the financial sector and there is erosion of medical ethics. There are irregularities in the academic field : some primary school teachers who continue to reside in towns and only "visit" their village schools occasionally, marks tampering at the higher levels of education and promotion of teachers on considerations other than merit. Similarly, there are irregularities in the sphere of public primary health care: primary health centres have their regular offices in the village and para-medics draw their salaries regularly, but many of these centres are rarely open for actual treatment. Many young and enthusiastic entrepreneurs feel that they cannot flourish without corruption and political connections. Again, take the case of the fiscal termites: in some states about one-third of the electricity consumption is not "billed", but treated as "transmission and distribution loss" – an euphemism for power theft. How can the State Electricity Boards which generate and distribute electricity become viable? In such a society, the emphasis on investment in education and health certainly reflects the right priorities. But corrupt practices such as those illustrated above abort returns to investment. How can any development plan, however well-designed, succeed in such a morally polluted environment? The issue of "governance", both at the private corporate level and the public sector level, which is receiving recently so much attention in development literature, loses much of its relevance in such an environment of pervasive corruption, both financial and moral.

The American case belongs to a somewhat different genre. In the light of recent developments, one is tempted to raise the question: is American capitalism crumbling? Revelations of corporate crookedness and accounting scandals have shaken the very foundations of American capitalist model. Corporate America's fall from grace is sudden and complete. The Enron, WorldCom and Xerox exposures have unveiled the ugly side of Western style capitalism under which, in the quest for short-term gain, wrong-doings are often overlooked. The collapse of Anderson, one of the

World's big five accounting firms has, in the wake of the Enron scandal, added a new dimension to the systemic infirmities. Fudging of accounts seems to have evolved into a fine art. This "Corporate-Accounting Firm-Capital Market" nexus has perhaps proved to be the last straw on the back of the American capitalist system. The depths of degradation to which unbridled corporate greed can lead has become all too obvious. These developments cannot be dismissed, as some apologists of American Capitalism seem to be doing as isolated incidents. As Professor Lester C. Thurow puts it: "The Enrons and WorldCom are not abnormalities in a basically sound system – Scandals are endemic to capitalism". As the post-Enron wave of corporate scandal swept America, Europe's response was that such a thing could not happen in Europe. But the Economist pointed out recently, that the Ahold Scandal showed that Europe is not immune from America's Corporate ills (*The Economist,* March 1st-7th, 2003).

In the case of Russia, the move from communism to capitalism after 1991 was supposed to bring unprecedented prosperity. It did not. A transition that lasted two decades during which poverty and inequality increased cannot be called a victory for capitalism. Even the IMF experts involved in facilitating smooth transition of Russia confess that the failure was "due in significant part to corruption".

These three typical cases are symptomatic of a sickness that afflicts the society, sickness born of moral pollution. Such sickness frustrates economic growth as in the case of India or Russia and/or erodes the quality of life as in the case of the US. If improvement in the quality of life is the end-objective of all development endeavours, the need to tackle this sickness becomes obvious.

Indian philosophy seems to offer a remedy for this sort of sickness. It advocates the need to build "development conscience" among all sections of the population, within a country and across countries. From times immemorial Indian philosophy has maintained that the all-round development of a society is best achieved through the betterment of the individual, which no doubt includes economic well-being but extends well beyond it. Social conscience must be inculcated among individuals through education at all stages and also professional training. All individuals must be sensitised, at their young age itself, to the abject poverty, the squalor, disease, ignorance and illiteracy that surround us. They must be made to begin to think in terms of what is our *dharma* or duty towards alleviating some of the infirmities that afflict our less fortunate fellow human beings. We may begin to think in terms of poverty within a nation and then extend it to poverty across countries. In fact, Indian philosophy regards the earth as one family: *"Vasundhaiva Kutumbikam"*.

One of the ancient scriptures of India, The *Bhrihadar-nyaka Upanishad* enjoins that our life must be guided by the following three *"Da's" "Damyata"*, that is, control yourself, *"Datta"* that is, give to others, and *"Dayadwam"*, that is, be compassionate. Thus, we must practice self-control, charity and compassion. Collectively these three characteristics constitute development conscience. Building up such conscience among all sections of the population – within a country and across countries – would go a long way towards accelerating economic growth, promoting a shared growth process, improving the quality of life and in general evolving a compassionate society.

At this stage it may be appropriate to recall the famous observation of the Noble Laureate Robert Solow: how often all discussions of the sources of growth and development seem to end in a blaze of sociology, which also explains the stubbornly large residuals in all growth accounting models. Our submission is that treating this factor as a "residual" is a major deficiency of all growth models. It is essential to treat "development conscience" as an essential ingredient of the development alchemy – in fact as a fifth factor of production. Some sceptics may raise the question: could this concept be quantified? The simple answer at this stage is that the utility of a concept does not depend upon the ease with which it can be quantified. At least a beginning could be made to incorporate the development conscience factor into the growth models, so that the growth process may be more meaningfully deciphired.

II

Monetary and Credit Policies

8

Suicide by Cutting Interest Rates

Monetary Policy: 2002-03

The financial scene is becoming curiouser and curiouser, as we approach April 29, when the RBI Governor, Dr. Bimal Jalan, is scheduled to announce the Monetary Policy for the first half of the financial year 2002-03. On the one hand, there is the clamour from the market that we should move towards a softer interest rate regime; the bank rate should be reduced from the present level of 6.5 per cent to say, 6 per cent and the cash reserve ratio (CRR) from 5.5 per cent to say, 4.5 per cent. A reduction of one percentage point in CRR means an injection of some Rs. 11,000 crore of liquidity in the banking system. Inadequate liquidity is not the problem of the banking system; it is excess liquidity.

The pertinent question to pose in this context is : how soft is soft enough?

On the other hand, look at the more recent developments. The RBI has successfully reduced the yield on 19-year government security to 7.7 per cent and on 10 year security to 6.85 per cent. The RBI was also able to siphon off excess liquidity of the banking system by raising more than Rs. 5,000 crore through its open market operations around these soft rates.

The prime lending rate (PLR) is well below 11 per cent but some banks are offering consumer loans, such as car loans, at 10 per cent. As for export credit, the effective interest cost on six-month rupee export credit, taking into account the forward premium on dollar, works out to 3 to 4 per cent, which is internationally competitive. Where then is the case for further reduction in the interest rate structure?

That banks are highly liquid is reflected in the fact that excess investments by banks – excess in the sense of above the level prescribed by the statutory liquidity ratio (SLR) added up to a staggering figure of Rs. 1,29,450 crore in October 2001. That was when the investment-deposit ratio was 38 per cent of the net demand and time liabilities (NDTL). This ratio has gone up further to 40 per cent in March 2002, clearly indicating that the magnitude of surplus investments has swelled further. Given such massive surplus liquidity, no wonder that banks continue to invest in government securities even after yields on them have declined sharply.

Thus, there is not only no rationale for a further reduction in interest rates but also, if such reduction is brought about through reduction in bank rate or in CRR, or both, it would be suicidal for banks and for the system as a whole. To the banks, because the average cost of funds is over 7 per cent in the case of public sector banks (PSBs) and hence, PSBs cannot go on investing in government securities with yields of just 7 per cent. To the system, because any further reduction in deposit rates – a necessary consequence of reduction in the bank rate – would erode the very foundations of the high saving phenomenon, that the PSBs have assiduously built over the years since the late 1970s.

In fact, by whetting the appetite of the PSBs for government stocks, the public debt management policy has rendered them practically dysfunctional, the credit-deposit ratio hovering around 50 per cent for the last couple of years. Even in March 2002, the ratio was at 52 per cent.

The April 2002 Credit Policy should take some positive measure to wean PSBs away from this addiction to investment in government securities. One possible option is to prescribe, either formally or informally, a ceiling on the PSBs, investment in government securities, say, 30 per cent of the NTDL. Only such a drastic measure can release banks' resources for supporting growth in the productive sectors.

The present *ennui* of PSBs can be traced back to the days when flawed public debt policy raised the maximum yield on 10-year government securities to an artificially high level of 14 per cent. The consequence of this was predictable. The PSBs found it convenient to invest the bulk of their resources in government securities – which are a zero-risk and zero transaction cost instrument, in preference to lending to the productive sectors. Thus, bank resources were diverted away from productive sectors to support government consumption. The rest is history. Such a high yield also set the tone for a high interest rate structure. The correction of this distortion was over-due but the RBI seems to have swung the pendulum to the other extreme.

The PSBs continuing to invest in government securities at yields of some 7 per cent is not sustainable because the average cost of funds to them is well above 7 per cent. If this situation persists, banks would perforce tend to reduce deposit rates further and this would prove disastrous for the system as a whole.

Historically, India graduated into a high saving phase in the late 1970s, thanks largely to the efforts of public sector banks to widen the banking system. In fact, bringing the rural and semi-urban segments of the economy into the fold of modern banking can be regarded a part of the economy's modernisation. Few developing countries can boast of a saving rate of, say, 20 to 25 per cent of GDP. Unfortunately, this strength is being eroded by the mindless pursuit of the soft interest rate regime that seems to be designed to benefit only the corporate elite. Even today, while car loans attract interest rates of 10 per cent, the small farmer continues to pay an interest rate of 12 per cent.

As a result of successive reduction in the bank rate and attendant measures, deposit rates have shrunk to a low of say, 7.5 to 8.5 per cent, impacting the savings rate at the macro level. Policy-makers now seem obsessed with replicating the American-style financial system on the Indian soil, oblivious of the fact that unlike in the American economy, the household sector in India accounts for the principal component of gross domestic saving. Any further reduction in deposit rates is, thus, bound to affect adversely the overall saving rate.

Additionally, last year there was the discrimination against banks in terms of fiscal treatment. While income from dividends – both from equity investments and from mutual funds – was exempt from individual income tax, interest income from bank deposits was subject to tax. The latter was also subject to tax deduction at source (TDS). This was one more instance of the contemporary policy-makers mimicking American-style promotion of the capital market. Despite all these sops the effort to develop the capital market was a colossal failure. Today, the capital market is in a shambles.

The Government has realised its mistake and removed this discrimination in this year's Budget. The scars of such discrimination are clearly visible. The rate of financial saving by households dipped to 10.5 per cent in 1999-2000 from 10.9 per cent in the preceding year. In the second half of the 1990s, the household sector financial saving rate has generally remained below peak of 11.9 per cent achieved in 1994-95. It is time the RBI took notice of this disturbing trend of deteriorating financial saving rate in the household sector which, in India, sets the tone for overall saving rate.

Apart from the saving rate being critical to investment and growth, savings assume other dimensions in developing countries. Lack of efficient credit and insurance markets makes household savings a critical determinant of welfare in developing countries.

Without savings, households have few mechanisms to smoothen unexpected variations in their incomes. Since saving is one of the few means of accumulating assets, the capacity to save becomes critical for increasing social mobility and enhancing future income-earning possibilities.

Thus, sustaining the present high rate of savings and, in fact, raising the saving rate further as envisaged in the Tenth Plan should become the paramount objective of macroeconomic management.

The Hindu Business Line, April 27, 2002.

9

Credit Policy: Different Thinking

The Credit Policy measures are remarkable for the following three reasons. First, the deftness with which Dr. Bimal Jalan muffled the enormous pressures built up by the corporate elite to reduce interest rates further; and what is more he has done it without offending the lobby. To appreciate the subtlety, one has to read between the lines of his 67-page statement.

Second, Dr. Jalan has, for the first time, come out openly with the confession that the Government's fiscal profligacy has, in effect, crowded out the productive sectors, so far as utilisation of banking sectors' resources is concerned. Though critics have been pointing out all along that the RBI has been an accomplice in the inglorious task of pre-empting the bulk of banking sectors' resources for the government borrowing programme, it is for the first time that the RBI has expressed its concern about the phenomenon in the following words:

> "...the overall monetary management becomes difficult when a large and growing borrowing programme of the Government, year after year, puts pressure on absorptive capacity of the market. Already, the banking system holds government securities of more than 38.5 per cent of the net demand and time liabilities as against the statutory minimum requirement of 25.0 per cent. In terms of volume, such holdings, above the statutory liquidity ratio (SLR) amounted to more than Rs. 1,40,300 crore which is higher than the gross borrowings of the Government. Such a large exposure to government securities may inhibit the ability of banks to meet the credit requirements of the productive sectors of the economy..."

In fact, this is the boldest statement of the decade by an RBI Governor. One hopes the RBI would continue to take follow-up measures to correct the distortion in the allocation of banking sectors resources between supporting government consumption and productive sectors of the economy. Dr. Jalan deserves to be congratulated on bringing the issue into the open.

Third, the pressure to bring down the lending rates further was being built up by the corporate sector, which is the most pampered sector, despite pretensions to the contrary. The effective interest cost to the Indian exporter, as the Governor's statement clarifies, works out to only 2 or 3 per cent taking into account the forward premia on the dollar. In contrast, the small farmer has to bear an interest cost of 12 per cent. Banks, particularly the foreign banks, treat the corporate sector as the only legitimate claimant of the banking sector's resources.

The RBI wittingly or unwittingly, lends credence to this popular myth. Take the following explanation of deceleration of non-food bank credit in 2001-02: "During 2001-02, non-food credit registered lower growth of 12.8 per cent (Rs. 80,411 crore) as against an increase of 14.9 per cent (Rs. 61,176 crore) in the previous year, reflecting deceleration in industrial production."

It is generally overlooked that such sectors as agriculture and small-scale industries are as important as industrial sector, in terms of their contribution to GDP, employment and exports. It is to Dr. Jalan's credit that specific measures have been taken to streamline the credit delivery mechanism to facilitate larger flow of credit to these non-industrial sectors. The limits for financing distribution of inputs for agriculture-allied activities, such as cattle feed, poultry feed, and so on, under the priority sector, have been increased to Rs. 25 lakh from Rs. 15 lakh. The limit of dispensation of collateral requirement for small-scale industry loans has been raised from the present Rs. 5 lakh to Rs. 15 lakh.

Another significant measure that has not received adequate attention is that the interest rate on loans to state governments under the rural infrastructure development fund (RIDF) has been reduced from 8.5 per cent to 6.5 per cent, that is at the bank rate. There has been enormous accumulation of resources under the RIDF, following successive Budget allocations. The Budget for 2002-03 provides another Rs. 5,500 crore. But the utilisation of these funds by the state government has been disappointing. It is hoped that the reduction in interest rates would be an incentive for better utilisation of these resources.

Had the RBI yielded to the pressures and reduced lending rates, this would have spelt disaster for the savings rate of the economy.

While not yielding to the pressure, the Governor has made the appropriate noises to pacify the pressure groups. In fact, the refrain that runs through the Governor's statement is: "RBI will continue to maintain current interest rate environment with a bias towards softer interest rate regime in the medium-term".

A concrete measure taken is the reduction of the cash reserve ratio (CRR) from 5.5 per cent to 5 per cent with effect from June 15, 2002. Even this measure is explained in terms of the RBI's medium-term objective of reducing the CRR to the statutory minimum of 3 per cent. This measure would result in replenishing banking sector's resources by some Rs. 5,500 crore. The bank rate for reducing which there was enormous pressure, remains unchanged. But, again, Dr. Jalan softens the lobby with the following sedative:

"In case the overall liquidity and credit situation warrants, and inflation rate continues to remain low, a reduction in the bank rate by up to half a percentage point (50 basis points) will be considered by the RBI as and when necessary. Normally, no central bank would like to reveal its policy intentions in advance but Dr. Jalan has tried a different tact.

The core issue of the banking scene for some years has been that public sector banks (PSBs) have become dysfunctional. The credit-deposit ratio of the banking system has been hovering around 50 per cent for some years now and this is not viable. PSBs seem to be content investing the bulk of their resources in government securities, which are zero-risk and zero-transaction-cost instruments. This has induced a sort of lending fatigue and agriculture, small-scale industries and even some small companies have been crying themselves hoarse that the PSBs are increasingly reluctant to lend to them. The RBI had maintained a studied silence on this crucial issue.

The mountain of excess investments in government securities to which Dr. Jalan referred for the first time stands as a monument of the lending paralysis by the PSBs and also the RBI's flawed public debt policy.

Though addressing the issue openly is, indeed, welcome, this is not enough. In fact, the RBI should think in terms of imposing on the PSBs a ceiling on their investments in government securities, say, 30 per cent of their net demand and time liabilities as against the prescribed limit of 25 per cent under the Statutory Liquidity Ratio (SLR) requirements.

Of course, such a ceiling can be implemented formally or informally. Only such a bold step could prod the PSBs to look at credit proposals from sector other than the corporate elite segment.

The savings habit so assiduously cultivated by Indian households since the latter half of the 1970s had received a severe felt in recent months by successive reductions in deposit rates and rates on small savings schemes and the public provident fund. There was a demand for reduction in the interest rate on savings accounts with commercial banks, which is fixed at 4 per cent.

Again the RBI has refrained from yielding to this demand. The RBI has explained that the effective rate on savings accounts works out to only 3.4 per cent, a rate too small to warrant reduction.

Few developing countries can boast of a savings rate of some 25 per cent of GDP and it is the household sector that contributes the bulk of financial savings. Any attempt to transplant American style financial system on the Indian soil, going by the market methodology, would prove counter productive. The RBI should continue its efforts to ward off any measures that would erode the saving habit.

The Hindu Business Line, May 9, 2002.

10

Credit Policy Imperatives

Correcting the Distortions

The Reserve Bank of India (RBI) is scheduled to announce, on October 29, what is conventionally known as the Busy Season Credit Policy for 2002-03. Misconceived policies of the more recent past have led to major distortions in the current monetary and credit situation and one hopes that the RBI would utilise the October policy to correct such distortions as the obsessive concern with ushering in a low interest rate regime, the inequitable interest rate structure and the obscenely massive borrowing programme of the government. These reflect the different dimensions of the distortion and correcting them should, therefore, become the October Credit Policy's imperative.

The finalisation of the Tenth Plan on October 3 by the Planning Commission adds yet another imperative to the Credit Policy – the institutional transformation of the credit delivery system. The Plan aims at raising the GDP growth rate from 6 per cent to 8 per cent. It also seeks to create 50 million jobs and reduce the poverty levels to 20 per cent of the population by the end of the Plan. Since the October Credit Policy would be the first meeting after the finalisation of the Tenth Plan, it behoves the RBI to address the question: are the present Credit Policy regime and the credit delivery system in consonance with the broad-based and decentralised growth implicit in the employment generation and poverty reduction targets? In the light of these considerations, the RBI should initiate policy measures to facilitate the anticipated pattern of growth.

Let us begin with the low interest rate regime. As a result of the mindless pursuit of low interest rates, perhaps inspired by the corporate lobby, the RBI has landed the banking system in an anarchy of interest rates. Although technically the prime lending rate is around 11 per cent, highly rated corporates are raising funds from banks at much lower rates: for instance, corporates access banks funds at 6 per cent through commercial paper (CP), or raise export credit at an effective rate of 4 per cent. Car loans can be accessed at 9 per cent. The banking system is highly liquid, with the credit-deposit ratio around only 52 per cent. There are too few corporate elites, or consumer loans, for too much bank money.

In sharp contrast, a small farmer has to pay an interest rate of 12 per cent. Equity considerations have been thrown to the wind. The RBI does not seem to appreciate adequately the adverse impact of such an ill-conceived low-interest rate regime on the macroeconomic management. Two such major repercussions need to be highlighted. First, the rates at which the Government borrows have come down drastically. For instance, the Government of India is able to raise money from banks at only 7 per cent through a ten-year government security. Thus, the RBI is encouraging fiscal profligacy. The Government is merrily borrowing such large amounts that it is crowding out the productive sectors of the economy.

It is to the credit of the RBI that in its April 2002 Credit Policy document it boldly exposed this distortion, in the following words: "...The overall monetary management becomes difficult when a large and growing borrowing programme of the Government year after year, puts pressure on absorptive capacity of the market. Already, the banking system holds government securities of more than 38.5 per cent of the net demand and time liabilities as against the statutory minimum requirement of 25 per cent. In terms of volume, such holdings, above the statutory liquidity ratio (SLR), amounted to more than Rs. 1,40,300 crore, which is higher than the gross borrowings of the government. Such a large exposure to government securities may inhibit the ability of banks to meet the credit requirements of the productive sectors of the economy..."

Since the yields on government securities set the tone for the interest rate regime, moving away from the low interest rate regime by raising yields on government securities becomes a Credit Policy imperative. If the RBI is ineffective in containing the overall dimensions of government borrowings, the least it can do is to raise the cost of borrowing to the government.

Perhaps, a far more powerful reason for the need to move away from the low interest rate regime is the adverse impact of the regime on savings. In India, the household sector is the largest single contributor to the total financial savings and bank deposits constitute the largest component of household sectors financial savings. Hence, deposits rates become critical to sustaining a high rates of overall savings. As a consequence of reducing lending rates, banks were compelled to bring down the deposits rates, which hover around 7 per cent today. Again, the interest income from bank deposits is subject to tax.

With the collapse of the capital market and mutual funds, including the UTI in disarray, individual savers are compelled to depend increasingly on bank deposits for investing their savings. If the current low deposit rates are allowed to persist in the medium-term, the savings of the household sector are bound to decelerate. India is among the few developing countries that can boast of a high saving rate which today stands at 23 to 24 per cent of GDP. It is pointless, therefore, to allow the erosion of household sectors savings just because we want to pamper the corporate elite.

At this point, one is reminded of the famous remarks made by Professor Rudi Dornbusch of MIT, though in a different context: "None of post-War expansions died of old age: They were all murdered by the Fed." Surely the RBI does not intend to share the honour of sabotaging savings, so assiduously built up over 1970-1990.

The RBI should, therefore, begin by raising yields on government securities and permit commercial banks raise their lending rates, so as to enable banks to raise their deposit rates. In the present context of a depressed capital market, this seems to be the only way to sustain the household sector's savings rate.

On the massive borrowing programme of the Government, the RBI has, at long last come out openly, but it should keep going at the Government to see fiscal light. There are four related aspects of the massive borrowing programme which need to be underlined.

First, the main burden of the government borrowing is falling on commercial banks and this is crowding productive sectors. Small savings have shown, in recent years, a healthy growth and hence they should continue to be supported, both by relatively higher interest rates and fiscal concessions. To the extent of their growth, the incidence of government borrowing on banks would be reduced.

Second, relief bonds were emerging as an important instrument for mobilising resources for government. Unfortunately, some restrictions have been imposed on them, thus restricting their access to individual savers. This is counterproductive. All such restrictions should be removed so that individual savers have unlimited access to relief bonds. This would also reduce the incidence of government borrowing on banks.

Third, despite the rhetoric of the RBI of developing the government debt market, players other than banks, have not emerged. Efforts should be made to bring in other players in the market.

Finally, developing a retail market in government securities – a theme which the RBI waxes eloquently – remains just tall talk.

It is pointless to destroy the well established institutional infrastructure for small savings and seek to build, in its stead, a non-viable retail market in government securities.

The October Credit Policy measures should at least reflect the RBI's initiatives in trying to resolve the internal contradictions in this financial segment.

Growth in the large and medium industries alone will not enable the economy to attain the targets of poverty reduction and employment expansion stipulated in the Tenth Plan. One has to depend upon decentralised and broad-based growth. Agriculture, non-agricultural employment in the rural sector, small industries, micro enterprises and a whole range of self-employment avenues – all these need to be supported.

This means that the moribund rural credit delivery system needs to be revitalised. It has now been accepted that one of the practical ways of reviving the somnolent rural credit system is to link banks, both commercial and cooperative, with self-help groups (SHGs) and non-governmental organisations (NGOs). Such a link would reduce transaction costs of rural credit institutions and also ensure good recovery.

The task of building the network of SHGs, NGOs, and microcredit institutions is gigantic and NABARD seems to be unequal to the task. Another area the RBI needs to explore is whether part of the huge stocks of foodgrains of more than 60 million tonnes with the Food Corporation of India can be used for generation of employment and income in the rural sector.

Could some sort of "Grain Loans" system be evolved to strengthen the entire rural credit delivery system? The modalities of harnessing surplus foodgrains for rural development need to be worked out.

All this calls for innovative approaches and, in this area, there are no models to copy from like the Basle norms for banking sector reforms.

In other words, the RBI must begin to spend in the coming years, an increasing amount of its time and talent on streamlining the rural credit delivery system; by transforming it appropriately.

The Hindu Business Line, October 22, 2002

11

Credit Policy

Symbolism is All

The core of the Monetary and Credit Policy measures *per se*, announced by Dr. Bimal Jalan, Governor, Reserve Bank of India, on October 29, constitutes only a very small part of the massive 70-page document embodying the Governor's statement on the Mid-term Review of Monetary and Credit Policy for 2002-03. Three measures constitute the core. First, the bank rate is reduced from 6.50 per cent to 6.25 per cent with effect from October 29. At this level, it is the lowest since 1973. Second, the cash reserve ratio (CRR) is reduced from 5 per cent to 4.75 per cent with effect from November 16. Third, the repo rate is reduced from 5.75 per cent to 5.50 per cent with effect from October 30. The rest of the massive statement of the Governor deals with operational matters, important though they are.

Taken together, the policy measures are nothing more than symbolic. In the first place, the changes are very small, by 25 basis points. Second, the changes are unwarranted in the current situation. For instance, the banking system is highly liquid today, with excess investment in government securities. While the statutory liquidity ratio (SLR) requirements are only 25 per cent of net time and demand liabilities, the actual investments add up to nearly 38 per cent.

With such liquidity, banks have little need to access RBI funds. Hence, the reduction in the bank and repo rates have become increasingly irrelevant to banks. The reduction in CRR is particularly irrelevant because, apart from the present excess liquidity, the demand for food credit is going to be negative this year in view of lower procurement and higher off-take of foodgrains.

During the current year up to October 4, food credit declined by Rs. 800 crore in sharp contrast to an increase of Rs. 10,200 crore recorded during the corresponding previous period. This massive reverse flow of funds from the food sector is going to swell the liquidity of banks further. If the RBI has not highlighted this point, it is perhaps deliberate.

As it is, the credit-deposit ratio is lower than 55 per cent and the decline in food credit will drive down the ratio further. Under such swelling liquidity, what purpose will the injection of another Rs. 2,500 crore into the banking system, which the reduction in CRR implies, serve? Only the RBI knows. Perhaps, it believes that symbolism is all.

If there is one hidden message these measures convey, it is that the low interest rate regime is here to stay. In macro terms, what is the impact of these measures on the economy? The immediate response of the stock market was positive, with the Sensex rising by 51 points or by 1.8 per cent to reach 2,885. But stock markets are not exactly known for rational behaviour and this may only reflect the announcement effect of the RBI measures. The economy as a whole may neither gain nor lose much, which underlines the symbolic character of the measures: not gain because the lending rates are already quite low. Although banks may, in the wake of these measures, symbolically again tend to reduce their lending rates marginally, as perhaps the RBI expects them to do, this is not going to have any positive impact on industrial growth. As it is, though the prime lending rate continues to be, say, 11 per cent, corporates are able to raise money from banks at much lower rates: for instance, at 6 per cent through commercial paper (CP), at an effective rate of 4 per cent for exports, 8 per cent through non-convertible debentures (NCDs) and at 9 per cent for car loans.

In fact, the Governor's statement is explicit about this point. Since banks are lending below their PLRs and have also reduced their maximum spread over PLR, the effective lending rates of banks have also shown some motivation. The sub-PLR lending of the banking system (excluding exports, the bulk of which is at sub-PLR) constituted over one-third of their total lending (Page 10). The scope for further reduction in further lending rates and such reduction making a positive impact on industrial growth is practically nil. Given this and the replenishment of banking sector's resources by Rs. 2,500 crore through reduction in CRR, there is no clear case for reducing deposit rates. However, public sector banks were quick to utilise this opportunity to reduce their deposit rates.

The State Bank of India has reduced its rates by 50 basic points: for instance, a three-year deposit would now attract 7 per cent interest, as compared to 7.5 per cent earlier. Other banks are likely to follow. This spiralling effect would affect the household sector savings, which account for the bulk of total financial savings of the economy.

The RBI was cautioned to guard against such an eventuality[1]. With the capital market in the doldrums and the UTI in disarray, the small saver had only banks to invest his savings. And now this avenue is also affected, one wonders whether it would erode the high saving rate of the economy in the medium-term.

On the one hand, the lowering of lending rates, even symbolically, would not help to boost industrial growth. On the other, there is the danger that if this interest rate regime persists in the medium-term, it may erode the savings rate. Even now it is not too late for RBI to keep a watch on the emerging situation and take appropriate corrective measures.

There is one area, which has not attracted much attention in the media, but in which the RBI has taken commendable initiatives – microfinance. The central bank deserves to be congratulated on these initiatives, which have to be seen against the objectives of the Tenth Plan. Three targets of the Plan assume importance in this context: GDP growth target of 8 per cent creation of 50 million jobs and reduction of poverty levels to 20 per cent of the population by the end of the Tenth Plan. Obviously, the growth of large and medium industries, even if it is sustained at, say, 8 per cent, would not be helpful in reaching these targets.

One has to look to agriculture, small industries, micro enterprises and non-farm employment in the rural sector. To support this decentralised and broad-based growth, there is a need to bring about institutional transformation in the rural credit delivery system. This is a task which was overdue, and the RBI has, at last, addressed it. In the coming years, the RBI would need to spend as much time on this transformation as it has been doing in banking sector reforms.

The Governor's statement on this theme quotes: "The Reserve Bank's objective was to accelerate the flow of bank credit to

1. Business Line, October 22, 2002.

microfinance institutions while maintaining their decentralised, voluntary and non-bureaucratic character."

"Accordingly, a number of initiatives have been taken by RBI. Comprehensive guidelines were issued to banks for mainstreaming microcredit and enhancing the outreach of microcredit providers. Banks were permitted to treat microfinance extended by them as part of their priority sector lending, banks were also allowed to classify their credit under SHG-Bank linkage programme as advances to weaker sections.

The SHG-Bank linkage programme has proved that banking with the poor is a viable proposition. It also benefited banks by extending the credit delivery process and ensuring more than 90 per cent recoveries besides being cost-effective."

"During the current year, 2002-03, the RBI plans a series of interactive sessions to review the progress made in this vital area and to put in place a more vibrant microfinance delivery environment in the country where complementary and competitive models of microfinance would be encouraged." (Pages 50 and 51). In more recent months, there were apprehensions whether the Monetary and Credit Policy measures were being designed to pamper the corporate sector alone. This initiative of the RBI in the area of microfinance would go a long way in correcting such an image. The financial system should respond to take larger concerns of the growth of the economy as spelt out in the plan.

Overall, the October Credit Policy measures touch only a small segment of the banking sector's problem. The core issues of the banking system continue to remain unaltered: the bulk of the public sector banks' resources being siphoned off to support government consumption at the cost of productive sectors of the economy and the RBI's inability to develop the public debt market with the result that public sector banks bear the brunt of government's borrowing programme.

The Hindu Business Line, November 1, 2002

12

Credit Policy

Sound, Fury and Substantive Issues

The Credit Policy package, announced on April 29, is calculated to create what one might call sound and fury, along with the other components to tackle substantive issues. The reduction of the Bank Rate from 6.25 per cent to 6 per cent and the cut in the Cash Reserve Ratio from 4.75 per cent to 4.50 per cent constitute the former component which has attracted, not unexpectedly, a good deal of media attention.

The macroeconomic conditions did not warrant these changes; there is a surfeit of liquidity in the banking system and the Reserve Bank of India (RBI) in its new-found love for the low-interest rate regime had already brought down the interest rates to historically low levels. But pampering the corporate sector has become one of the main compulsions of political economy since the 1990s phase of liberalisation and financial sector reforms. The changes in the Bank Rate and the CRR may be regarded as yet another step that the Monetary Policy has taken to bow to the new compulsions.

Responding to the RBI signals, some major banks have already announced the reduction in their primary lending rates (PLRs). The corporate sector never had it so good. While admittedly rhetoric – and these charges are no more than that – is part of the policy-making games, the RBI seems to be oblivious to the deleterious impact that such low-interest rates would have, in the medium-term, on savings. The collapse of the UTI and the moribund capital market have already shocked the household sector.

The other component, which is less glamorous, is the activist role that the RBI has at long last resumed playing in prodding banks, particularly public sector banks (PSBs), to cater to sectors other than the industrial sector. It may be recalled that the new banking culture, nurtured by economic and financial sector reforms, had induced even PSBs to focus on three Cs – Consumer credit, Corporate elite, and Capital market-related activities. Every PSB wanted to cast itself in the image of foreign banks. To lend to agriculture, small-scale industries and the self-employed segment became infra dig.

But this illusion was shattered by the capital market becoming moribund: several non-banking finance companies (NBFCs) withering away; bridge loans, and lending to brokers becoming scarce; merchant banking activities coming to a halt; and mutual funds of many PSBs winding up. In the case of lending to corporates, too many banks chased too few 'A' rated companies. In the case of consumer lending, a sort of saturation point was reached.

It was in this kind of a bind that the PSBs found the soft option of investing the bulk of their resources in government securities, and the RBI, as the manager of public debt, encouraged this tendency. Otherwise, how does one explain the fact that the maximum yield and government securities soared to an absurd level of 14 per cent at some point? The disastrous results of this confluence of factors are all too obvious. Against the prescribed level of 25 per cent of deposits, the PSBs today invest some 39 per cent of deposits in government securities.

The RBI Governor's Credit Policy statement refers to the medium-term objective of reducing the CRR to 3 per cent, in justification of the present cut by a quarter per cent. One wonders what happened to the Narasimham Committee's prescription of reducing the statutory liquidity ratio (SLR) to 25 per cent. Although technically the SLR has been reduced, actual investments have continued to remain around 38 per cent. The Governor is obviously conscious of this distortion in the deployment of banking sector's resources but has so far done precious little about correcting the distortion.

The Governor's assessment is very clear: "...overall monetary management becomes difficult when a large and growing borrowing programme of the Government puts pressure on the absorptive capacity of the market. The banking system already holds government securities of about 39 per cent of net demand and time liabilities (NDTL) as against the statutory minimum requirement of 25 per cent. In terms of volume such holdings above the statutory liquidity ratio (SLR) amounted to Rs. 1,95,974 crore in March 2003 which is much higher than the gross borrowings of the government. Further, such a scenario exposes banks to substantial interest rate risk which has adverse implications for sustained financial stability. In addition, the increasing interest payments have raised concerns about the sustainability of a large public debt. A reduction in fiscal deficit would release resources for infrastructure and industrial financing, which in turn would help in realising the long-term potential of the economy..."

From the macroeconomic point of view, what is most disturbing is that such a huge amount of nearly Rs. 2,00,000 crore is being diverted away from supporting productive sectors to underpin government consumption – consumption, because the Government of India incurs a large deficit on its current revenue account. This trend, which has become a chronic feature of PSBs, can be characterised as a sort of 'sickness' of the PSBs for which the RBI has also to share a part of the blame.

It is against this broader perspective that the following measures announced on April 29 assume significance; credit for drip irrigation, housing finance in the rural and semi-urban areas, and microfinance credit to dealers in drip irrigation/sprinkler irrigation system/ agricultural machinery, irrespective of the location of the dealer, has been brought under priority sector lending. Similarly, direct finance to housing in rural and semi-urban areas, which is part of priority sector lending, has been further liberalised; now banks can lend up to Rs. 10 lakh for this purpose. In the new architecture of the rural credit system, microcredit institutions would play a critical role and it is only since 1999 that the RBI has begun to pay attention to this segment of the financial sector.

Microcredit institutions and self-help groups have been recognised as important vehicles for generation of income and delivery of credit to self-employed persons. Intellectual leadership for promoting this segment can come only from the RBI and not NABARD, which is ill-equipped to deal with such innovative approaches. It is gratifying to note that the RBI, which had adopted a stand-off attitude towards the rural credit system all along the 1990s, has woken up to the fact that the system has become moribund.

These RBI initiatives are indeed welcome. Banks have been advised to provide maximum support to SHGs. The banks SHGs-linked credit programme is a success story. Recently, the RBI had "a wide-raging interface" with a cross-section of microcredit providers. Pursuant to these interactions, four informal group have been set up by the RBI to look into various issues relating to (i) structure and sustainability, (ii) funding, (iii) regulators, and (iv) capacity building for microfinance delivery. The RBI, according to the Credit Policy, will discuss the recommendations of these informal groups in a wider forum for possible implementation.

Taken together, these measures reflect the RBI's concern for dealing with the substantive issues: how to prod the PSBs to begin to lend more to the rural sector, and to dissuade them from exercising the soft option of investing the bulk of their resources in government securities. The credit-deposit ratio of banks has been hovering around 50 per cent for the last several years, reflecting the new 'sickness' of the PSBs, and the RBI should spare no efforts to curve this ailment.

The banking system, particularly the PSBs, must reinvent itself by looking beyond the private corporate sector, and these measures of the RBI would enable banks to do so. As it is, the corporate sector is doing well for itself, with export growth as high as 18 per cent and industrial growth inching back to nearly 6 per cent. The flow of bank credit to the industrial sector has greatly improved in 2002-03, with non-food credit registering a very high growth of nearly 18 per cent. The Governor's statement provides a wide-ranging list of particular industries to which the size of credit flow has been increased. Neither the availability nor the cost of credit seems to pose any problems for industrial and export growth. Perhaps, in an unguarded moment, the Governor's statement confesses that there was no need for further softening interest rates: "On balance of probabilities, given normal conditions and overall stability in macroeconomic environment, in view of several structural constraints, the present nominal and real interest rates are relatively low. There may not be significant potential for further sizeable downward movement in interest rates."

That is how one should separate the rhetoric of Credit Policy from the substantive issues we have referred to above. Another substantive issue with which the RBI has merely tinkered is the cooperative credit structure. In the light of the recent scams in some urban cooperative banks, the RBI has now directed that urban cooperative banks "with immediate effect should not grant loans and advances (both secured and unsecured) to directors, their relatives and firms/concerns/companies in which they are interested".

The question really is why such loans were permitted in the first place? Did the RBI had to wait for the JPC recommendations to act on this issue? The broader issue is that the entire cooperative credit system is in a mess. The cooperative movement has lost its elan of the late 1950s and the 1960s. During this phase, the intellectual leadership for the movement originated largely from the RBI but when the portfolio of agricultural credit was transferred to NABARD, the RBI almost washed its hands off this responsibility.

NABARD is simply not equipped to provide such guidance at the macro level. The cooperative credit system today is rudderless, let alone setting a future course.

This role needs to be redefined and a road map for modernising the system drawn up. The scope of the cooperative credit system in the context of decentralised development through panchayati raj institutions (PRIs), its relationship with micro-credit institutions, with the private sector – all these need to be re-worked out. It is time the RBI appointed a high-power committee to draw up a blueprint for cooperative development.

Finally, the RBI needs to do much move to prod the PSBs to reach out to the rural sector – both farm and non-farm segments. Perhaps, the RBI may think in terms of imposing, formally or informally, a ceiling on the PSBs investment in government securities, say, 30 per cent of their NTDL. Only such a drastic action could provoke the PSBs to reaching out to sectors other than the three 'Cs' mentioned above.

The Hindu Business Line, May 13, 2003

III

Banking and Savings

13

What Ails Co-operative Banking?

Co-operative banks are in the news again, but not for the right reasons. It may be recalled that during March 2001, some Urban Co-operative Banks (UCBs) faced liquidity and insolvency problems. A major underlying factor was non-adherence by these UCBs to prudential norms prescribed by Reserve Bank of India (RBI). These included lending to stock brokers exceeding prudential exposure norms to single party/group and the limit on unsecured advances.

At the centre of the problem was what the RBI calls a multi-state scheduled UCB, which witnessed a sudden withdrawal of deposits. If the share market was the theatre of the scam in 2001, it is the government debt market which is the theatre of the present scam. An intermediary was successful in inducing some co-operative banks to part with large sums on the pretext of buying government securities for them, without really purchasing such securities. What is disturbing is that not only UCBs but some district central co-operative banks were also involved in this disastrous affair. Why this new-found love for government securities, even by district co-operative banks? The RBI seems to be content with merely *ad hoc* responses.

For instance, in the aftermath of the 2001 scam, the RBI put a stop to lending by UCBs, directly or indirectly, against security of stocks. Such *ad hoc* responses, no doubt, plug the loopholes but they cannot stop the system from opening up other loopholes. This is what perhaps happened in 2002. The point is that the infirmities of the co-operative system are more serious than what these periodic scams seem to expose. The co-operative credit structure today is directionless, with the RBI having diluted its earlier commitment by transferring the subject of rural credit to NABARD. The intellectual leadership for shaping the future of the co-operative credit system can come only from the RBI while, no doubt, NABARD can discharge its responsibilities regarding the routine operation. The central bank can have a vision about the nature of the future growth of the economy and so shape the financial system as to support the anticipated pattern of growth. Only on the basis of such a macro picture could the relative roles of different segments of the financial system be defined.

For instance, what sub-sectors of the economy are co-operatives expected to support? What is the role of the Regional Rural Banks (RRBs)? How do the microcredit institutions, which we are more recently attempting to build, fit into the whole business of rural development? The RBI should have a broad idea of the relative roles of the financial segments and guide their development accordingly. Various committees conducted in-depth studies recently of different aspects of the co-operative credit structure. Madhavarao Committee on UCBs (1999); Jagdish Capoor Task force on Co-operative credit system (2000), and V.S. Vyas Group on Rural Credit (2001). Unfortunately, none of these groups addressed the basic issue. It is time that the RBI takes up the task of providing a blueprint of the future shape of the rural credit delivery system.

Today, the co-operative credit system neither has the leadership of men such as Vaikunth Lal Mehta or D.R. Gadgil; nor the guidelines of the RBI. It is in this sense that the co-operative system remains directionless and falls an easy victim to rapacious elements which are on the look out for such a prey.

Super-imposed on this fact is the impact of the new banking culture, nurtured by banking sector reforms co-operative managers want to imitate Public Sector Banks (PSBs) which, in turn, want to cast themselves in the image of foreign banks. The emphasis now is on a "quick kill" rather than on extending medium and long-term credit to productive sectors. For instance, banks had enough resources to extend bridge loans to enterprises such as M.S. Shoes, but they had no funds to support the production of sugar in Maharashtra. No wonder this culture has also percolated to the management of the co-operative financial institutions. Bereft of the co-operative ideology of yesteryears, corrupted by the hard banking culture, it is no wonder that scams are manifesting themselves in the co-operative banking institutions with regular frequency. It is a matter of grave concern that the financial health of a large number of co-operative credit institutions is extremely 'fragile', to borrow a phrase from the RBI. It is time that the co-operative financial system reinvents itself in terms of what it could do to promote employment expansion, especially for the small man, promote broad-based growth and reduce poverty. The exaggerated emphasis placed by both Government of India and the RBI on the development of the capital market during the reform phase, seems to be at the root of many recent scams: the mushrooming growth of non-banking financial companies (NBFCs) and their eventual collapse, the Harshad Mehta episode and the recent stock market disturbances.

Goading PSBs to involve themselves increasingly in the stock market, fiscal concession for investors in equity and in mutual funds are some of the artificial props given to boost the capital market. Today, even the RRBs are allowed to invest in bonds of the public sector units (PSUs). Facilitating the reverse flow of funds from the rural to the urban areas is the most retrograde step that policy-makers have taken. Priority sectors – including agriculture, small industry, retail trade, the whole range of non-farm activities in the rural sector – have no access to the capital market and hence the emphasis should be to promote flow of resources from the urban to the rural areas. The RBI itself admits that "The objective of co-operative banking is to create enduring and sustainable financial institutions which remain responsive to the credit needs of weaker sections" (Report on Trend and Progress of Banking in India, 2000-01). In spite of the artificial props, the attempts to develop the capital market has been a dismal failure, as the phenomenal growth of the private placement market clearly demonstrates.

On the other hand, the capital market has become the incubator for financial scams. It is, therefore, necessary to keep the co-operative banking system as far away as possible from the capital market.

It is not adequately appreciated that the co-operative financial segment occupies a crucial position in the financial system in terms of its reach and volume of business. Credit co-operatives account for 70 per cent of the rural credit outlets. Rural co-operative banks account for about 30 per cent of total rural deposits and 44 per cent of outstanding loans and advances of the banking system in respect of agriculture and rural development. UCBs are expected to mobilise savings from the middle-and low-income groups and extend credit to priority sectors and weaker sections.

While we have failed to reduce poverty levels during the last 50 years since the inception of planning in 1950s, China was able to reduce its poverty levels to a minimal of 6 per cent of the rural population in just two decades. Two features of such an astonishing performance need to be highlighted: faster agricultural growth of 5.2 per cent per annum and an explosion in non-farm employment. Rural industry grew rapidly employing about 25 per cent of the rural labour force. Town and village enterprises (TVE) have expanded at a fast rate, contributing about 40 per cent to the total industrial output.

The architects of the Tenth Plan recognise the imperative need of broad-based, decentralised growth as is clear in the following statement. "It is important to emphasise that the equity-related objectives of the Plan, which are extremely important, are linked to the growth objectives, and the attainment of one may not be possible without the attainment of the other.

For example, high rates of growth are essential if we want to provide a sufficient expansion of sustainable high quality employment opportunities to the expanding labour force and ensure a sufficient increase in income of the poor and the disadvantaged. (Draft Approach Paper to the Tenth Plan – 2002-2007)

Empirical experience of the Asian tigers has shown that shared growth is sustainable growth. This is especially so in India where expansion of employment opportunities has to necessarily come from sources other than the organised large-scale sector. If thus decentralised, broad-based growth is the desired objective, it is important to facilitate such growth through appropriate financial mechanisms in this task; PSBs, RRBs, the whole range of co-operative credit institutions and micro credit institutions would all have to participate. It is the business of the RBI to broadly earmark the respective areas on which each of these institutions could focus and also device ways and means of establishing appropriate links among the institutions.

The Hindu Business Line, June 26, 2002.

14

Banking on Commercial Banks

Public sector banks went through a traumatic phase in the 1990s, when banking sector reforms based on the Basle norms were implemented. Over the years, the public sector banking system had become a huge, inert animal which moved only when prodded by the Reserve Bank of India or the Government. This is no longer so, with PSBs today responding promptly to market signals. This remarkable metamorphosis is reflected in the profile of the PSBs which emerges from *RBI's Report on Trend and Progress of Banking in India, 2001-02*. The RBI deserves to be commended on this highly analytical report, which clearly demonstrates the resilience of PSBs.

"During the year 2001-02, there was a significant improvement in the profitability of the scheduled commercial banks (SCBs) owing to the rise in trading profits attributable to the soft interest rate regime, coupled with the containment in operating expenses, notwithstanding the higher provisions and contingencies..." There was a healthy growth of time deposits, despite the significant lowering of interest rates on deposits. What is more, there was a perceptible decline in non-performing assets (NPAs). The ratio of gross NPAs to gross advances of SCBs declined from 11.4 per cent at end-March 2001 to 10.4 per cent as at end-March 2002. Net NPAs to net advances declined from 6.2 per cent to 5.5 per cent, over the same period.

Most important among the prudential norms introduced by the RBI to strengthen the banking system is the capital to risk-weighted assets ratio (CRAR). At end-March 2002, 25 PSBs had CRAR exceeding the stipulated minimum of 9 per cent — only two accounting for 4.3 per cent of total assets of PSBs, did not fulfill the stipulation.

On the whole, the picture seems to be quite encouraging, especially in the context of a scenario where most analysts take pleasure in debunking PSBs. The recent passing of the Securities and

Reconstruction of Financial Assets and Enforcement of Securities Bill, by Parliament, should further strengthen PSBs. Since this legislation provides more powers to banks to recover their dues from their borrowers, it should go a long way in reducing NPAs significantly.

It, thus, becomes clear that the macro environment in which the PSBs function is not exactly conducive to enhancing their efficiency. Three features of this macro environment may be indicated. First, the sub-optimal use of banking sector's resources : at end-October 2002, the credit-deposit ratio of the SCBs was only 54 per cent. In any healthy and vibrant commercial banking system, the ratio would be 70 to 75 per cent. Second, the PSBs are bearing the brunt of the heavy borrowing programme of the government. At end-October 2002, the investment-deposit ratio was more than 41 per cent in contrast to the stipulated statutory liquidity ratio (SLR) of only 25 per cent. In other words, government borrowings are crowding out the productive sectors.

Obviously, the first and second features are mutually-related. The third stems from the objectives of the Tenth Plan : among the important objectives are, creating five million jobs and reducing poverty to 20 per cent. These objectives cannot be achieved by merely focussing on large and medium industries and exports, as the current policy seems to be doing. The thrust of growth would have to be also on agriculture, small industries, microenterprises, self-employment avenues and, generally, on what is referred to as the decentralised sector. What should be the strategy to reach out to the decentralised sector? This is the issue which the RBI needs to address.

Profits: Myth and Reality

Net profits of PSBs recorded a huge jump from Rs. 4,317 crore in 2000-01 to Rs. 8,301 crore in 2001-02. Market theologists may exult in this sharp rise, attributing it to deregulation of the banking sector. That would be a hasty conclusion. There is a catch in this: the bulk of the profits are attributable to the bonanza of the low interest rate regime. For instance, of the total net profits of Rs. 8,301 crore in 2001-02, nearly Rs. 6,000 crore was due to trading in government securities. Another Rs. 1,547 crore came from forex transactions. Pure banking transactions could claim little profits. In fact, in the case of some banks such as Indian Bank, if trading profits are assumed as zero, they would be in the red.

Deposits Growth

There is a similar analytical point in the explanation for the buoyant deposits growth. Time deposits growth at 15.9 per cent in 2001-02 was only marginally higher than the deposits growth of 15.8 per cent last year. In fact, deposits growth become really buoyant this year : growth in time deposits, up to October 4, at 13.8 per cent was significantly higher than the growth rate of 10.8 per cent recorded during the corresponding previous period. The RBI's explanation of the buoyancy phenomenon is rather superficial: "The steady accretion to time deposits with banks, despite the downward movement in interest rates, reflects the safe heaven sentiments..."

The real explanation lies in the fact that with the collapse of the UTI, and with the stock market in the doldrums, the saver, particularly the small saver, is returning to the banking system. One would have thought that with the relatively lower GDP growth anticipated in 2002-03, deposits growth would have decelerated this year. If this has not taken place, it is because alternative investment avenues have become far less attractive. The "return of the prodigal" kind of thesis seems to offer a more appropriate explanation.

It is necessary to reiterate that fiscal policy should not discriminate against bank deposits, as the Task Force has proposed. Exempting dividend income from personal taxation while taxing interest income from bank deposits is counterproductive in the Indian context. Commercial banks, particularly the PSBs, play an important role in development, as the capital market. Recently, the RBI had asked PSBs to extend medium- and long-term credit to projects. One hopes that a level-playing field between bank deposits and investment in equities would be maintained.

Sliming of the PSBs

Another dramatic transformation which has not attracted much attention, is the sliming of PSBs. The major component of operating costs for commercial banks is the Wage Bill, which witnessed a decline of 6.2 per cent in 2001-02. Twenty-six out of the total 27 PSBs introduced a voluntary retirement scheme (VRS) in 2000-01 and, as a result, there was a reduction in staff strength by about 12 per cent. This has had a salutary effect on improving the profit parameters of banks. With the lowering of wage costs, the ratio of wage bill to total assets of the SCBs fell from 1.8 per cent in 2000-01 to 1.4 per cent in 2001-02. Obviously, such a reduction will have a continuing salutary impact on operating expenditure of the PSBs.

Overall, the PSBs appear to be resilient institutions that have developed an ability to respond to market signals. They have shed fat and adjusted themselves remarkably to a low interest rate regime.

Admittedly, the enormous profits made in 2001-02 was because of a fortuitous factor and, therefore, should not be misconstrued as an indicator of efficiency. The low interest rate regime brought about a sharp decline in yields on government securities, say from 14 per cent on a 10-year security to 7 per cent. And this provided profitable opportunities for trading in government securities and the rest is history.

What is now important is that the policy-makers must realise that the growth of PSBs is as important as the development of the capital market. The policy discrimination against PSBs and in favour of the capital market, which is clearly visible throughout the 1990s, must end. Bank deposits and investment and inequities must enjoy a level-playing field so far as fiscal concessions are concerned. Even if the capital market develops – and this is a heroic assumption in the present moribund state of the stock market – it cannot reach the decentralised sector, the development of which has assumed greater importance in the Tenth Plan. Fortunately, the RBI is taking greater interest in developing the microcredit institutions. The thrust of the RBI policy in the coming years should be to evolve a network of PSBs, microcredit institutions, cooperatives, RRBs, NGOs and self-help groups (SHGs) to strengthen the credit support to the decentralised sector. Banking on commercial banks for achieving the Tenth Plan objectives, including sustaining a high rate of savings, should thus become the *Mantra* of both fiscal and monetary policy.

The Hindu Business Line, December 3, 2002.

15

UTI, Small Savings and Financial Crisis

"The UTI should, as a matter of principle, not offer a guaranteed rate of return under any scheme even for one year. Such guarantee is the very antithesis of a mutual fund".

"The UTI should curb its enthusiasm to raise the dividend sharply".

"The US-64 is quite clearly the flagship scheme and it is here that the UTI faces its acid test. The Deepak Parekh committee gave an outer limit of three years for the scheme to go over to NAV basis. It would not be necessary to await the Malegam Committee report before moving on to an NAV".

"The UTI is meant to be the fund manager par excellence and the gilt market is by far the largest segment of the financial market. While the UTI has moved towards entering the field of financial services, it has missed the bus by not recognising that it should have been one of the first applicants to become a primary dealer (PD) in government securities — better late than never!"

All these are embodied in the article, 'Repositioning UTI', included in an anthology of 51 that form the book, *Twists and Turns of Financial Reforms* by the former RBI Deputy Governor, Dr. S.S. Tarapore. The book makes a remarkable contribution to the analysis of the current financial issues.

Had the UTI heeded his advice, it could have avoided the present fiasco. The freezing of repurchases in May 2002 under its flagship scheme US 64, the declaration of zero dividend on the US 64 in June, and also zero income under the Monthly Income Plan (MIP) 2000 initially, and modified later to 3 per cent which is, incidentally, lower than the rate of interest on savings accounts offered by banks — do all these actions drive the last nail in the coffin of the Indian capital market? One wonders.

The UTI fiasco is accompanied by the sharp reduction in the interest rates on small savings. Commercial banks have also dropped their deposit rates to the lowest levels. This mindless pursuit of a "low interest rate regime", disregarding its macro implications, has brought about a sort of financial crisis. The logic underlying the reduction in interest rates on small savings that they represent "high cost borrowings" is flawed. High interest burden on the government is due not so much to the high cost of borrowing as the alarmingly high magnitude of borrowings. Fiscal profligacy is the real culprit and fiscal profligacy is interest-neutral. It is important for policy-makers to unravel the macro implications of the financial crisis brought about by the UTI fiasco and the reduction in interest rates on small savings, and take appropriate policy correctives.

In any case, the Indian capital market is in a moribund state. For the last couple of years, it has been able to raise hardly Rs. 5,000-6,000 crore per year. In contrast, the private placement market has assumed gigantic proportions, raising some Rs. 60,000 crore per year. This itself is an indictment of the whole lot of measures taken by the Government and the RBI to promote the capital market. These measures include wooing foreign institutional investors (FIIs) to the portfolio investment market, fiscal incentives, such as the exemption of dividends from individual income tax goading public sector banks (PSBs) to involve themselves increasingly, both directly and indirectly, in the capital market: have all these measures come to a nought?

The story does not end with the betrayal of its millions of investors by the UTI. Following the recommendation of the Dr. Y.V. Reddy Committee on administered interest rates, that on small savings were also reduced drastically. Small savings occupy a unique position in the economy. Broadly, three types of small savings are available: postal deposits, saving certificates, and social security schemes, such as the Public Provident Fund and retirement schemes. While postal deposits are akin to bank deposits, the others are medium-term instruments designed for specific purposes.

Unlike in such developed countries as the US and the UK, where some such schemes do operate, in India, resources mobilised by small-savings schemes constitute a significant proportion of the household sectors' financial savings. For instance, the share of small savings as a percentage of net financial savings of the household sector rose from 7.9 per cent in 1996-97 to 13.8 per cent in 1998-99. The Reddy Committee advocated market-determined interest rates on small savings, which according to it, "are high cost borrowings" for the government.

Little was the other side of the coin appreciated — the household sector that would be adversely affected by the drastic reduction in interest rates on small savings. Interest rates on bank deposits, which are another important avenue for household sector's savings, have already touched the lowest levels. The so-called "low interest rate regime" has, thus, dealt a death blow to household income and savings.

This sudden decline in the income of households that save and invest, and the decline in interest in small savings would have far-reaching implications at the macro level. This phenomenon and the currency crisis of 1997 in East Asia, though not strictly analogous, share some common elements.

Economies that experienced the sharpest currency depreciation suffered the deepest cuts in real wages. To some extent, families smoothed their incomes through increased labour participation and private transfers. Though the evidence suggests that wealthier families were better able to smooth consumption.

The initial impact was on the urban corporate sector, but rural households were also affected and, in some instances, suffered deeper losses than the urban families. Such currency crises have been typically short-lived but whether households that plunged into poverty during a crisis are able to recover as the economy recovers, remains an open question.

Admittedly, the Indian financial crisis was induced, unlike the currency crisis, by domestic policy initiative. But its impact on other segments of the economy may not be totally dissimilar. In the currency crisis, of course, there is a direct impact on GDP, especially if exports play an important role in the economy concerned.

In the case of the financial crisis of the Indian type, there is no direct adverse impact on GDP, in the immediate run. But in the medium term, GDP may be adversely affected through the decline in savings and investment. In any case, policy-makers ought to unravel these macro implications of the financial crisis.

Take the impact of the financial crisis, which implies loss of confidence in the financial institutions, on the behaviour of savings.

The Tenth Five Year Plan seeks to raise the gross domestic savings from the base level of 26.3 per cent of GDP to 29.6 per cent, and the household sector's savings from 19 per cent to 19.4 per cent (Draft Approach Paper to the Tenth Five-Year Plan, 2002-2007). How does the present financial crisis change the picture?

At the micro level, aggregate data mask considerable churning in its effect on households incomes across different income-groups. Some households nearly totally dependant on interest and dividend incomes may be forced to dis-save. What should be the policy stance in such cases? Making up the loss of income through increased labour participation is simply not an option available in India, given the tight employment situation.

More important, the rationale for reduction of interest on small savings is not sustainable. The real reason of high interest burdens on public debt is not so much in "high cost of borrowing" as the alarmingly large size of borrowing itself. Fiscal profligacy is the real culprit and fiscal profligacy is interest-neutral. Policy-makers should, therefore, focus on restoring fiscal prudence.

India is one of the few developing countries that can boast of high level of savings and, hence, sustaining this high level of savings should be the over-riding objective of macro economic management. Misguided policies based on narrow considerations should, therefore, be corrected without further delay.

The Hindu Business Line, July 23, 2002.

16

The UTI in Retrospect

At a time when many experts are ready to write the Unit Trust of India's obituary, it is courageous of Mr. V.G. Pendharkar – the first Executive Trustee of the UTI – to write its history. Mr. Pendharkar, 87, deserves to be commended for producing an excellent book, *Unit Trust of India: Retrospect and Prospect*. However, it is not surprising that he is sad at the recent developments which have made UTI a moribund institution.

Mr. Pendharkar provides interesting insights into the evolution of the UTI, the subtle power game between the Centre and the Reserve Bank of India, and the role of "foreign experts" and other lobbies in weaning the UTI away from its original objectives. Does such history have any lessons for shaping the future of the UTI? One is not sure. Mr. Pendharkar stops short of sketching a road map for the UTI's recovery. One hopes that he will address this issue in his next book.

Mr. Pendharkar begins with the uniqueness of the UTI. Though established in 1964 by an Act of Parliament, neither did the Government of India own it nor contribute any capital. The RBI was asked to contribute one-half of its initial capital of Rs. 5 crore, and given the mandate of running the UTI in the interest of the unit-holders. The State Bank of India and the Life Insurance Corporation contributed 15 per cent of the capital each, and the rest was contributed by scheduled commercial banks which were not nationalised then. This kind of structure for a unit trust is not found anywhere else in the world. Again, unlike other unit trusts and mutual funds, the UTI was not created to earn profits.

Today, where market-faddism rules supreme, it is necessary to re-emphasise this original objective of the UTI. Mr. Pendharkar writes: "In the course of nearly four decades of its existence, it (the UTI) has succeeded phenomenally in achieving its objective and has the largest share anywhere in the world of the domestic mutual fund industry." The emergence of a "foreign expert" during the setting up of the UTI makes an interesting story. The announcement by the then Finance Minister that the Government of India was contemplating the establishment of a Unit Trust caught the eye of Mr. George Woods, the then President of the World Bank. Mr. Woods took a great deal of interest in the Indian financial system, as he was one of the principal architects of the ICICI, in which his bank, First Boston Corporation Bank, had a sizeable shareholding. Mr. Woods offered, through Mr. B.K. Nehru, who was India's Executive Director on the World Bank, the services of an expert.

The Centre jumped at the offer, and asked the RBI to hold up the finalisation of the Unit Trust proposals till the expert visited India. Mr. Pendharkar's reaction to this will make Indians proud. "I was not too happy about it, as I did not think it was beyond our capabilities to set up a Unit Trust and run it on our own. In my view, the offer typified the low estimate Westerners had about our abilities. But what surprised me, not only in this case but in several others, was that even our own people do not have faith in our officials."

The story of the foreign expert does not end here. Mr. Pendharkar goes on to elaborate with his tongue in cheek. "The expert, Mr. Sullivan, a retired senior official from one of the middle-sized mutual funds in the US and a personal friend of Mr. George Woods duly arrived with his wife in late October 1963, and spent a fortnight in the country. They were a charming couple with old-world manners and very much interested in archaeology. We were very glad to take them to places of archaeological interest, such as Kalva caves, Elephanta, Ajanta, Ellora and so on, which they wished to see. After his return from these visits, Mr. Sullivan discussed with me our draft proposals to establish the Trust in the public sector."

The only point Mr. Sullivan made was that the provision to limit the ownership of units to individuals might result in unnecessarily restricting the market for units. While making this point, he had in mind the practice in the US, where small pension funds are an important class of customers for the Unit Trusts. Though Mr. Pendharkar did not agree with this view, the Centre accepted the foreign expert's suggestion, and the necessary amendments were made in the draft Bill. Thus began corporate investment in the UTI, which received a boost from the tax concession given by the Government in the 1990-91 Budget. According to this concession, the dividends received by a company from investments in other companies, including the UTI, were completely exempt from corporate income tax, provided the dividends declared by the investing company were higher than the dividends received.

The result was a phenomenal increase in corporate investment which accounted for 57 per cent of the total capital under US-64 scheme. Because of high liquidity the corporate sector used the UTI to park its liquid funds. This added to the volatility of the UTI funds. The corporate lobby which perhaps subtly opposed the establishment of the UTI in the public sector made use of it for its own benefits later. The Government-RBI power game started with the finalisation of the UTI charter itself. The RBI draft of the UTI charter stipulated that the Chairman will be nominated by it, and one more nominee would be on the Board of Trustees. While finalising the Draft Bill, the Centre changed this stipulation. The Chairman was to be nominated by the Government, albeit in consultation with RBI. Mr. Pendharkar explains: "In a subtle way it makes the Chairman dependent on the Government. Although the appointment was to be made in consultation with the Reserve Bank, the Government could appoint a person of its choice as Chairman even if the Bank did not approve of him. Consultation does not imply approval. Moreover, it is an established convention that the appointing authority is also the disciplinary authority." It is obvious that government authority does make room for political and bureaucratic meddling. Would things have been different, if the UTI were to function under the RBI umbrella? One wonders.

That raises the broader question of privatisation, which is being bandied about as a panacea for all economic evils. This is not correct. Mismanagement is ownership neutral. Mr. Pendharkar believes that the UTI should continue to operate in the public sector and, perhaps, autonomy is the best solution. Even in the case of public sector banks, the Narasimham Committee pleaded for greater autonomy. But today privatisation is the buzzword and nobody bothers about autonomy. Mr. Pendharkar makes a fervent plea for reviving the US-64. "It is quite clear that public interest is involved here. If there is no chance of reviving the US-64, it will mean that a million investors from the low and middle income groups will be financially ruined. This would be most undesirable and public interest demands that some effective steps should be taken to avoid such a calamity."

Investors can only hope that Mr. Pendharkar's plea is heeded to.

The Hindu Business Line, December 20, 2002.

17

Small Savings and Market Mythology

Small savings occupy a rather unique position in the Indian scenario. Broadly, three types of small savings schemes are in operation: postal deposits, saving certificates, and social security schemes, such as the Public Provident Fund (PPF) and retirements schemes. While postal deposits are akin to bank deposits, the others are medium-term instruments designed for specific purposes. Unlike in developed countries like the US and the UK, where some such schemes do operate, in India resources mobilised by small savings schemes constitute a significant proportion of the household sector's total financial savings. For instance, the share of small savings as a percentage of net financial savings of the household sector rose from 7.9 per cent in 1996-97 to 13.8 per cent in 1998-99. In fact, in the 1990s gross collections from these schemes have grown at a phenomenal rate of 17 per cent per annum, compared with bank deposit growth of around 13 per cent. Gross collections rose from Rs. 18,920 crore in 1990-91 to Rs. 75,542 crore in 1999-2000. In other words, small savings appear to have imparted an element of dynamism to financial savings growth, over the period. It may be recalled here that the phenomenal expansion of commercial banks, both in terms of widening and deepening of the banking system, in the early 1970s was responsible, to a considerable extent, for enabling the Indian economy to graduate into a high-saving economy in the latter half of the 1970s ('The High Saving Phase of the Indian Economy', occasional papers, RBI, June 1980). Was such a role being played by small savings in the 1990s? It is necessary to raise this question because savings are critical to development; in fact, Arthur Lewis defined development simply as a process of converting a 5 per cent saving economy into a 12 per cent saving economy. The Tenth Plan seeks to raise the gross domestic savings from the base of 26.3 per cent of GDP to 29.6 per cent, and the household sector's savings from 19 per cent to 19.4 per cent (draft approach paper to the Tenth

Five-Year Plan, 2002-2007, page 11). What role should be assigned to small savings in this effort of further raising India's savings rate?

One looks in vain for answers to such macroeconomic questions in the report of the expert committee to review the system of administered interest rates and other related issues (Chairman: Y.V. Reddy, September 2001). After all, the question of interest rates on savings cannot be considered in isolation from the overriding objective of achieving a higher savings rate. Instead, one is treated to a rhetoric on the market mythology, and to a distorted view of small savings as a source of financing fiscal deficit.

The starting point of the committee's deliberations itself is flawed: "However, the real interest particularly for borrowers is still perceived by industry and commerce as high" (p.6). The logic seems to be that the corporate elite wants cheaper funds from banks and hence reduce the deposit rates. Who bothers if this will have an adverse impact on the household sector's savings? One gets the general impression from the committee's deliberations that the sole function of banks or the financial system generally is to provide cheap finance to the corporate sector. Every other objective must subserve this overriding objective. Secondly, the committee seems to have assumed the role of *messiah* of market-determined interest rates. Administered interest rates are anathema to it: "Last but not the least is the administered interest rates on small savings which makes the structure of interest rates inflexible downward" (p.7). Again, "Regulation of interest rates in this segment has not only created distortions in the interest rate structure but has also adversely affected the allocative efficiency of resources" (Introduction). The faith of the committee in the allocative efficiency of market-determined interest rates is, as we would seek to show, textbookish and does not reflect ground realities. The overzealous effort of Indian policy-makers to move towards a market-determined interest rate structure has resulted in the anarchy of interest rates (*The Business Line*, April 21, 2000).

Today, while highly rated corporates or multinational corporations (MNCs) can easily raise money from banks at, say, 9 per cent through commercial papers (CPs), or non-convertible debentures (NCDs), the small farmer has to bear an interest rate of 12 per cent. In addition, the corporate sector enjoys fiscal concession:

the cost of interest is treated as deductible expenditure – a concession not available to sectors like agriculture. Furthermore, the new banking culture, nurtured by reforms, aims at a 'quick kill'. Banks have enough funds to provide bridge loans to enterprises like M.S. Shoes, but they have no funds to support the production of sugar in Maharashtra. Even now, the credit target for agriculture of 18 per cent of net bank credit remains unfulfilled. Even at the international level, this textbookish belief in the allocative efficiency of market-determined interest rates is being questioned. As Dani Rodrik puts it forcefully, "It takes too much blind faith in markets to believe that global allocation of resources is enhanced by the twenty-something-year-olds in London who move hundreds of millions of dollars around the globe in a matter of an instant..." (*The New Global Economy and Developing Countries: Making Openness Work*, Johns Hopkins University Press, Baltimore, 1999).

Thirdly, the committee's stress is on small savings as a major source of financing fiscal deficit; and not on the contribution of small savings to the household sector's total savings. The share of small savings in the financing of combined gross fixed deficit (GFD) of the central and state governments rose from 17 per cent in 1990-91 to 20 per cent in 2000-01 (p. 25). Since small savings "are high cost borrowings for the government" (p. 12), the interest on small savings must be reduced. Strange logic indeed! The committee seems to overlook the fact that, historically, small savings were designed primarily to inculcate the habit of thrift among the middle and low-income groups, particularly in the rural and semi-urban areas. If governments, both at the centre and in the states, began to treat them as sources of deficit finance, it is a distortion. Instead of recommending the correction of this distortion, the committee seeks to perpetuate it by recommending reduction in interest rates on such savings. The committee contradicts itself by making the following statement. "In view of these, there is an urgent need for reforms in the sector with a view to putting in place a suitable mechanism for the productive use of these resources for the long-term gain of stakeholders" (p. 12) and one could add, for the long-term gain of the economy, as a whole. The committee would have acquitted itself admirably, if only it had made the plea of governments: "Leave the small savings alone".

Instead of pontificating on the high cost of borrowing, through small savings, to the central government, the committee could have tackled the heart of the problem, namely, the fiscal profligacy of the central government, with the Reserve Bank of India (RBI) acting as an ungrudging accomplice in facilitating government profligacy. Take the case of commercial banks, the investments by whom in the Government of India's securities far exceed prescribed levels. While the prescribed statutory liquidity ratio (SLR) is 25 per cent, the actual investment – deposit ratio of banks is 38 per cent. In other words, excess investment – excess in the sense of above the prescribed norms – in government securities by banks adds up to a staggering Rs. 1,28,460 crore as of October 2001. Thus resources on a massive scale are being diverted away from productive sectors to support government consumption. Viewed against this background, it becomes clear that small savings are only a minor episode in the general drama of fiscal profligacy.

The committee is apparently oblivious of the profligacy. This is reflected in its recommendation that the entire net proceeds from small saving collected after March 31, 2002 should be transferred to the state governments. In the same breath, the committee recommends that since the central government would have no share from collections after March 2002, the market borrowings programme of the central government should be enhanced to the extent of the liabilities (p. 47). The committee has missed an important opportunity to inject a degree of fiscal responsibility into the central government.

Such massive borrowings by the central government also has important implications for interest rates and this fact exposes the market mythology of interest rates around which the report of the committee is woven. It may be recalled that only a couple of years ago, the maximum yield on government securities had risen sharply to 14 per cent and it is with great difficulty that the RBI has managed to bring it down to 11 to 11.5 per cent recently. These interest rates set the tone for the interest rate structure as a whole. The committee's recommendations that the interest rates on small savings should be anchored in the rates of various instruments of government borrowing makes hardly any sense. For instance, the committee recommends that the interest rate on one-year postal deposit should be benchmarked to the average yield of 364-day treasury bills, or that the interest rate on five-year postal deposit may be benchmarked to the average secondary market yield on government securities having a residual maturity of around five years (p. 45). Such fluctuating yields – which in any case do not reflect the true market rates because of various factors conditioning the secondary market in government securities – only add an element of uncertainty to the small and rather unsophisticated investors in small savings instruments and thus affect their growth adversely. A periodic review and realignment of all interest rates on small savings is perfectly in order and such readjustment does impart flexibility – both upwards and downwards – to the interest rates. Linking these interest rates to borrowing instruments of government is bad in theory and may prove counterproductive in practice.

That the committee lacks a development perspective is further corroborated by the fact that nowhere does the report discuss the question of streamlining small savings schemes with a view to enhancing their reach. Could the post office, particularly in the rural and semi-urban areas, be converted into a mini-banking institution in order to enhance its total volume of business? RBI has recently taken up the task of strengthening microcredit institutions. Could some link be established between resources mobilised through small savings schemes and microcredit institutions, by providing appropriate safeguards? Ironically, RBI waxes eloquently on its intention to develop a retail market in government securities at a time when the secondary market in government securities is itself still not developed, even in metropolitan centres. What is the rationale for ignoring the well established network of mobilising small savings? This is one more example of an amazing perversion of priorities in financial sector reforms.

Economic and Political Weekly, January 19, 2002.

18

Bank Shares, Capital Market and Governance

The issue of return of capital by public sector banks, that had got the stock market in lather, is to be taken up in the monsoon session of Parliament, especially the aspects of pricing. After the upheaval in the market, the Finance Ministry had, in June, asked the Securities and Exchange Board of India (SEBI) to probe into the price volatility of some PSB shares during April-June 2003. And according to SEBI, which submitted its report on June 16, the sharp swings in share prices were the market's response to different statements made by the Finance Ministry on the issue of return of capital to government by some PSBs. The circle is, thus, complete.

This unhappy episode, which saw some investors make losses, should be viewed in a broader perspective: the inherent tendency of the capital market to create and exploit fully speculative opportunities and the lack of good governance on the part of the Finance Ministry. If only had the Ministry spoken in one voice or maintained a studied silence on the issue of return of capital by PSBs, this episode would perhaps have not occurred at all.

At the outset, one must distinguish between the underlying medium-term trend in bank share prices and the purely speculative bout of rise and fall in prices. Share prices of PSBs firmed up in the medium-term because of the improvement in fundamentals. For instance, in 2001-02, there was a significant jump in PSB profitability owing to a decline in the wage bill, an improvement in trading profits and a fall in non-performing assets (NPAs).

For PSBs, the reduction in wage costs on account of the voluntary retirement scheme (VRS) introduced in the previous year was Rs. 1,881 crore. To optimise utilisation of human resource, 26 of the 27 PSBs introduced the scheme, which resulted in a 12 per cent reduction in staff.

Second, trading profits – buying and selling government securities – attributable to the softer interest rate regime jumped from Rs. 2,250 crore in 2000-01 to Rs. 5,999 crore in 2001-02.

Third, NPAs as a percentage of advances declined from 15.8 in 1998-99 to 13.9 in 1999-2000 and to 12.3 in 2000-01. Thus, the operating profits of PSBs zoomed by 57 per cent over the previous year. PSBs have been helped in their recovery of dues/NPAs by the re-promulgation, on August 22, 2002, of the Securitisation and Reconstruction of Financial Assets and Enforcement of Security Interest Ordinance by the Central Government. The ordinance provides certain benefits to banks in the area of realisation of loans and advances and some PSBs, at least, have made good use of the legislation.

These three factors have together helped improve the bottomline of PSBs and this was reflected in rising share prices of most PSB. For instance, the Bank of India share rose from Rs. 110 in 2000-01 to Rs. 133 in 2001-02 and that of Corporation Bank from Rs. 110 to Rs. 133. Internationally, such sustained rise driven by fundamentals is normal as far as the banking sector is concerned.

What is worrisome is the erratic and sharp swings in share prices engineered by speculators – a phenomenon which has little to do with fundamentals. And the volatility in prices in April-June belongs to this genre. In such cases, it is the speculator who gains and genuine investors, particularly the smaller ones, lose out.

The capital market, the world over, is a strange animal. While it serves as a useful instrument for mobilising capital for entrepreneurs, it also acts as a breeding ground of financial scams, of various hues and sizes.

As Prof. Lester C. Thurow of the Sloan School of Management at MIT puts it: "The Enrons and WorldComs are not abnormalities in a basically sound system". Scandals are endemic to capitalism.

The current episode has to be seen in this perspective. It does not relate to all PSBs but to only those that have tapped the capital market. These PSBs should have established a good track record for them to be able to attract private investment.

Historically, PSBs were grossly undercapitalised. The prevalent view at the time was that as they were government-owned, their viability was not in question.

But with financial sector reforms and in the context of applying the Basle norms to Indian banks, it became necessary for the Government to inject large doses of capital into PSBs to help them meet the capital adequacy norms.

There is nothing wrong if some of the PSBs, especially those that have been doing well and able to raise capital in the market, want to return part of the Government's capital. But the catch here is: if some PSBs did plan to return part of the capital, would the shares be valued at par or at prevailing market prices?

In fact, the shares of Punjab National Bank, Bank of Baroda and Oriental Bank of Commerce hit the roof from end-April through May based on rumours that these banks would return their equity to the Government at par. If this had happened, it would obviously have improved the earnings per share of all non-government holders of these shares.

The subsequent movements in the prices of these shares reflected the market's response to statements by the Finance Ministry. The statement on May 28 that shares would be bought back at par boosted the prices. But the one on May 30 that shares would be bought back at market prices depressed the prices. And, on June 3, it was stated that no decision had been taken on the issue and this added to the confusion.

The fact is non-issues have been trumpeted by speculators to make a fast buck. There is no reason why the Government as a shareholder should be discriminated against. The Finance Ministry should develop a nose for such market rumours and should have scotched the subsequent not-so-serious developments in one voice.

This is the essence of good governance. Internally, there could be differences in the approaches to solving problems, but these should have been sorted through internal discussions before airing views to the public.

In retrospect, it is now clear that such varying views have impacted the market, by causing losses to some genuine investors and gains, of course, to speculators. The Finance Ministry has been blamed for inordinate delays in appointing PSB heads and even executive directors. Good governance requires that the lines of successions are clearly drawn up so that there is no uncertainty about the constitution of the top management.

The current episode has added another dimension too, that is, in a market-led economy, when banks are partly owned by the government, the Ministry should become market savvy.

Also, the policymakers must be provoked to consider whether it is desirable to promote the return of bank capital to the government. For instance, it is possible to visualise a situation wherein the Government's share in bank capital keeps declining from, say, 51 per cent to 33 per cent without any capital necessarily being returned back to it.

That is, individual banks may enlarge their capital base by raising larger resources from the market. The objective of reducing the Government's share, as set out by the Narasimham Committee, may be achieved without going through the traumatic experience of the current episode.

Perhaps, managing the banking system when PSBs were fully owned by Government was much simple. Governance in the new market-led regime is far more complicated and it is time that all policymaker concerned became market-savvy.

The Hindu Business Line, July 15, 2003.

19

IDBI: Yielding to Bureaucratic Pressures

The metamorphosis of the Industrial Development Bank of India (IDBI) provides a sad case study of how a vibrant and dynamic financial institution can be emasculated by bureaucratic meddling and thoughtless policies. Indian policy-makers of the reform era have by now established a high reputation for faithfully following IMF prescriptions and adopting "international best practices", irrespective of their relevance to the India-specific socio-economic milieu. All subsidies are bad and, hence, the Reserve Bank of India discontinued since 1992, its Long-Term Operations (LTO) Fund, through which the IDBI used to obtain concessional funds for on-lending to industries at concessional rates of interest. This was a mortal blow to IDBI's operations, since it had to depend on the market for its source of funds.

The RBI, at one time, raised the interest rates to usurious levels by providing the maximum yield on government securities of 14 per cent. Obviously, in this high interest regime, the IDBI could not raise money from the market and sustain its operations. In fact, this episode should be viewed as part of the larger story of IMF/World Bank strategy of de-emphasising development banking and over-emphasising the development of the capital market.

Perhaps the lobby of the fund-managers of the developed countries had succeeded in converting IMF/World Bank to their view of developing capital markets in emerging economies. If the capital markets in the emerging economies do not develop rapidly, because of the success of development banks in these countries, where would they invest profitably their massive surplus funds? Thus, the IMF/World Bank may have had their own reasons for subtly changing their strategy in favour of capital markets and against development banks.

Indian policy-makers should have resisted this pressure. Perhaps, few of the present day policy-makers remember the excellent track record of the IDBI. Many of the large and medium industrial houses of today owe their growth, expansion and success to the IDBI. Internationally, the IDBI had acquired such an image that some countries sent in their experts to study its profile so that it could be replicated in their own country.

On reflection, one feels that during these initial years, the professionals who headed the IDBI had a sense of commitment, enjoyed a measure of independence, and perhaps asserted it too. To the bureaucracy, finance was a new world and it was feeling its way leaving the professionals to run the show. This congruence seemed to have worked well for IDBI's health and growth. In the subsequent years, perhaps the tentacles of bureaucracy spread deeply and the last straw was the financial sector reforms patterned on the IMF/World Bank model.

On the impact of reforms, as a whole, on the financial system, I would reiterate that "The financial sector reforms, introduced in the 1990s as part of the process of liberalisation and globalisation of the Indian economy, have, in effect, succeeded in alienating the financial system from the business of development."

Today, the IDBI may be said to have become dysfunctional with net non-performing assets (NPAs) as high as 14 per cent and fresh lending practically tapering off because of resource constraint. In fact, reforms have been a double failure in the sense that they have failed to revive the capital market. Despite all the artificial props given to support the capital market through fiscal and banking incentives, it is in a moribund state. In the early 1990s, when the capital, raised through new issues, averaged around Rs. 10,000 crore annually, the expectation was that fresh capital raised would soar to an annual level of Rs. 50,000 crore. In sharp contrast, the average annual level of fresh capital raised has shrunk to some Rs. 6000 crore in more recent years.

The culture nurtured by reforms has yielded some interesting by-products. The State Bank of India, when it wanted to appoint its economic adviser, chose to advertise for the positions in *The Economist*, London. The ICICI appointed a superstar as its brand ambassador, at a hefty price. It became fashionable for public sector financial institutions to engage "foreign consultants" like Pricewaterhouse Coopers and Arthur Andersen to advise them on restructuring, and the IDBI was no exception. The tons of reports of management consultants must be now lying in the archives of IDBI. In the post-Enron fire and brimstone, perhaps nobody would like to go back to them now.

Nobody has provided the rationale for de-emphasising the role of development banks in emerging economies. Let the capital market develop autonomously but this development need not be exclusive of strengthening the development banks. Similarly, all subsidies are not bad. The overall benefits accruing from the promotion of development banks would more than compensate the cost of subsides. There was thus no case at all for the RBI to discontinue its concessional assistance to the IDBI through the LTO facility. Similarly, there is no case for providing artificial props to the capital market and for discriminating against development or even commercial banks.

It is against this broad canvas that the various proposals to restructure the IDBI need to be assessed. The Parliamentary Standing Committee on Finance is reported to have cleared the repeal of the IDBI Act and recommended the corporatisation of the institution and its conversion into a bank. The converted bank would concentrate on lending to the corporate sector and hence would not do any retail banking. What is commendable is that the Committee has stressed that IDBI's focus on development should be retained. The converted bank would thus be not like any other bank catering to the corporate elite but its operations would be guided by the development philosophy. That is where the relevance to the India-specific issues assumes importance. Otherwise, in today's India, the corporate elite is much pampered, with both foreign and Indian banks chasing them. The banking system is characterised by excess liquidity with the credit-deposit ratio hovering around 54 per cent. In this situation, it is the borrower – particularly the highly-rated corporates – who calls the tune.

If the new converted bank is to play its development role effectively, two pre-conditions seem necessary: autonomy and cheap resources. The Narasimham Committee had identified official meddling as one of the important factors responsible for the deterioration of the performance of public sector banks. This seems to hold true for IDBI too. A large measure of autonomy in the running of the new bank would go a long way towards ensuring its efficiency. In terms of professional competence, Indian bankers – both development and commercial – are second to none, and given the right environment, they can produce the desired results. There is thus, a strong case for separating ownership and management in respect of both commercial and development banks. Perhaps, a board comprising eminent persons may help in creating the right environment. Second, the RBI should revive its LTO facility to provide concessional resources to the new bank. Even in the soft interest rate regime, there are segments of the economy which warrant a preferential treatment, and the new banks can cater to them only if they have access to cheap funds.

The reshaping of individual financial institutions or the architecture of the financial system as a whole should be guided by visions of the future pattern of industrial growth. In this context, the recent experience of China, another success story of development, is illuminating.

An important insight that can be gained from the Chinese experience is that there was an explosion of non-farm employment during the two decades (1978-1998). Rural industry grew sizeably employing about 25 per cent of the rural labour force. Township and Village Enterprises (TVE) expanded rapidly during the reform era, contributing about 40 per cent to the total industrial output.

Access to credit, subsidies credit at that, was one of the important factors which facilitated such rapid growth. Has this experience of the Chinese miracle any lessons for India?

The crux of the matter is that the corporate elite, at this point of India's industrial development, is a pampered segment, with both the foreign banks and public sector banks wooing them.

The highly-rated companies are able to raise resource effortlessly at rates of interest much lower that what a small farmer is required to pay for his bank borrowing. They have also access to external commercial borrowings. In terms of future growth of the industrial sector, the need seems to be to facilitate larger flow of credit, both short-term and long-term, to the smaller corporates, small industries, micro enterprises and industries in the rural sector.

Admittedly, the new converted bank may not do retail banking but it could act as a think-tank in terms of considering how best to spread the financial infrastructure to facilitate broad-based and decentralised industrial growth. Perhaps, acting as an apex bank, it could also extend financial and technical support to the wide range of financial institutions directly involved in financing smaller industries.

The new bank would thus be not just another commercial bank catering to large industries – which it would no doubt continue to do – but it would also play an active development role.

The Hindu Business Line, July 24, 2003.

IV

Utilisation of Forex Reserves

20

Forex Reserves

Use them to Revitalise the Economy

The package of measures announced by the Finance Minister, Mr. Jaswant Singh, on January 10, 2003, is hailed by many as a big leap forward towards full convertibility of the rupee. The measures, among others, include the following:

- Indian residents – individuals, corporates, and mutual funds – are permitted to invest in the equities of companies listed in recognised overseas stock exchanges.

The only condition here is that these companies should have a shareholding of at least 10 per cent in a company listed on an Indian stock exchange.

Interestingly, there is no ceiling on individual investments abroad. In contrast, there is a collective ceiling of $1 billion on mutual funds' investments and a limit of 25 per cent of net worth on corporate investment;

- Indian companies with branches overseas can acquire immovable property abroad for business and staff residence purposes; and
- Up to $1 million of proceeds from assets transfer in India can be remitted abroad.

The whole package makes one wonder whether the country has become so affluent in foreign exchange resources as to warrant a throwing open of the floodgates.

This unbridled liberalisation is rather premature. At the time when the IMF, the vocal advocate of total convertibility, is cautioning emerging economies to hasten slowly towards capital convertibility, the path that India has chosen is one where even angels would fear to tread.

The only plausible interpretation is that it is a panic reaction to the mounting forex reserves, which have crossed $70 billion. If gold imports had not been liberalised, the reserves would have risen further by, say, another $20 billion.

Export growth this year, at nearly 20 per cent, has been buoyant, and policy-makers perhaps apprehended that the rising trend in reserves would persist. The soft option they have chosen is to throw open the exit door to forex reserves. This is unfortunate because there are several areas, such as infrastructure and power, which need large doses of forex.

The measures do not seem to have been well-thought-out either. There seems to be an element of recklessness. For instance, the Tarapore Committee on Capital Account Convertibility had also advocated liberalisation of capital transfers, but in stages. They recommended that individuals be permitted to invest abroad limited amounts – starting at around $25,000 and rising to $100,000.

The current measures envisage unlimited investments. If the Government and the RBI want to permit such capital transfers, why the convoluted conditionalities? Individuals can only invest in specified companies, but the Government has not published the list of eligible ones. Does it expect small, individual investors to conduct their own research to identify such companies?

Again, does the Government expect that this measure would prompt foreign companies to list themselves on Indian stock exchange and raise their shareholding in Indian companies to 10 per cent? Individuals cannot invest their funds with banks abroad in interest-bearing deposits, nor in debt instruments. Fortunately, mutual funds are eligible to do so. Thus, for the uninitiated, it is difficult to understand the rationale behind the conditionalities.

One thing that is clear, though, is that the Government has not, despite pretensions, grown out of the regulatory syndrome. The "unlimited freedom" given to individual investors is an illusion.

It would have made more practical sense if the Government had followed the Tarapore Committee recommendation, of imposing a ceiling on individual investments, but giving investors total freedom to invest in any instruments of their choice. Exchange control is not to be used to achieve multiple objectives.

The current exchange liberalisation is not confined merely to the capital account. NRIs, for instance, were thus far permitted to remit a total of $230,000 a year. In the new regime, there is a quantum jump in the ceiling; an omnibus limit of $1 million has now been placed without any sub-ceilings.

The country has for long been wooing NRIs, inducing them to bring in more foreign exchange by, among other things, exempting from tax their interest income from bank deposits and so on – resident Indians have to pay taxes on interest income. And now, if NRI remittances are not that important because of the comfortable forex position, why continue with the tax concessions? And why pamper the NRIs by inducing them to take out larger amounts of forex?

The fact is, there is not even a medium-term policy of macro management of forex reserves. Hence, the accumulation of reserves has become an embarrassment to the Government, just as the mountain of foodgrain stocks in FCI godowns has.

For a developing country, it is prudent to maintain only a reasonable level of forex reserves – equivalent of, say six months' imports. More reserves than this would be unproductive because, in the final analysis, this would imply lending the same to developed countries such as the US, the UK or Germany at cheaper rates of interest.

The average import bill has been around $50 billion in the last three years. Hence, it would have been prudent to maintain, on an average, reserves of, say, $25 billion. Right from March 1997 the reserves were higher than this level. From March 1998 onwards they have been rising consistently, touching $58 billion in June 2002. The recent spurt in reserves is history. Efforts should have been directed towards utilising a part of these for financing import of capital or intermediate goods, which would have boosted the country's domestic production. These goods could then have been used to develop, say, the power or transport infrastructure. Why not salvage the Enron power project through a public sector undertaking (PSU)? There is little evidence of either the Government or the RBI thinking on these lines. On the contrary, they seem to be in a great hurry to get the state out of all economic activity.

If a policy on macro management of forex resources were in place, the internal contradictions would not have emerged. On the one hand, NRIs and foreign institutional investors (FIIs) are wooed to bring in forex resources and, on the other, private corporate entities and even public sector undertakings are being encouraged to go in for foreign commercial borrowings.

Why did the country raise such huge foreign loans through Resurgent India Bonds? Obviously, the costs of borrowing from abroad are always higher than the returns on our investments in developed countries.

The least that can be done now is to reduce the foreign liabilities by utilising part of the forex reserves. Similarly, the incentives, by way of fiscal concessions to NRI investments in India, should be trimmed. Instead, the Government seems bent on frittering away valuable forex through half-baked ideas on exchange liberalisation. It is time a comprehensive policy on macro management of foreign reserves was put in place.

The Hindu Business Line, February 6, 2003.

21

Capital Account Convertibility

Challenging the Underlying Philosophy

There was a time when moving towards capital account convertibility was regarded as a mark of a developing country graduating into a developed country. This conviction also formed part of the IMF/World Bank theology. All this has changed now, with the 1990s experience challenging the underlying philosophy. Massive volumes of capital moved into East Asia and Latin America and then abruptly the flow reversed. At a moments notice, hitherto successful economies plunged into deep recession. The *London Economist* sums up the contemporary wisdom on the subject: "For many developing countries, unrestricted inflows of capital are an avoidable danger."

It goes on to add: "Untidy as it may be, economic liberals should acknowledge that capital controls – of a certain restricted sort, and in certain cases – have a role." Even the IMF, which once advocated, with a missionary zeal, movement towards total convertibility on capital account, now cautions developing countries to hasten slowly.

These are some of the random thoughts which occur to us while ruminating on the book by Dr. S.S. Tarapore entitled *Capital Account Convertibility, Monetary Policy and Reforms,* published recently. The volume brings together 31 lectures delivered by Dr. Tarapore on capital account convertibility, monetary policy, financial sector reforms and fiscal policy. The book makes a major contribution to the current thinking on the broad area of financial sector reforms and provides useful inputs for future policy-making.

The Committee on Capital Account Convertibility, which was appointed in 1997 with Dr. Tarapore as chairman, had provided a road map for the economy to move towards full convertibility step by step, and the time-frame was 1997-2000. The Committee had also laid down certain pre-conditions for implementing the reforms. But nothing much happened during this phase. Then, came the phase subsequent to 1999-2000 when there was a phenomenal increase in foreign exchange reserves of more than $41 billion cumulatively. In 2002-03 alone, there was a quantum jump in reserves by $21.3 billion. This significant improvement in the external position is, to quote the Reserve Bank of India (RBI), "unprecedented in India's history".

The total reserves soared to $73.5 billion towards the end of April 2003 and it is anticipated that the level may touch $100 billion in the not-too-distant future. Perhaps, it is this embarrassingly high level of reserves which swept the policy-makers off their feet and the soft option they chose was to liberalise both the current and capital account exchange control regime. Thus, we moved towards capital account convertibility not so much because of the intellectual support provided by the Tarapore Committee as by the compulsions of the foreign reserves affluence.

This conclusion is further corroborated by the fact that the pre-conditions stipulated by the Tarapore Committee for moving towards full convertibility were not fulfilled. What were the pre-conditions?

A look at three of them. First, in terms of fiscal consolidation, the Committee had stipulated that gross fiscal deficit, as a percentage of GDP, should be reduced from the budgeted level of 4.5 per cent in 1997-98 to four in 1998-99 and further to 3.5 in 1999-2000. In reality, the gross fiscal deficit, as a percentage of GDP, stood at 5.9 in 2002-03 and even in 2003-04 the percentage would go down to only 5.6.

Second, the mandated rate of inflation for the three-year period 1997-98 to 1999-2000 should be an average of 3 to 5 per cent. The annual inflation rate, based on the wholesale price index (WPI, Base 1993-94), averaged at 4.7 per cent during the three-year period 1999-2000 to 2001-02.

Third, the gross non-performing assets (NPAs) of banks, as percentage of total advances, should be brought down in phases to 12 per cent in 1997-98, to 9 per cent in 1998-99, and to 5 per cent in 1999-2000.

In reality, the gross NPAs of public sector banks, as a percentage of total advances, declined from 16 per cent at end-March 1998 to 11.1 per cent at end-March 2002, that is nowhere near the stipulated levels. Thus, going by the pre-conditions laid down by the Tarapore

Committee, the economy was not mature enough to move towards capital account convertibility.

At this point, although it is a diversion, one must record the appreciation of the transparency of the RBI. The data and information quoted above to compare the stipulated targets with the actuals are provided by the RBI itself in its *Report on Currency and Finance, 2002-03* (page VII-22).

The ineptness of policy-makers and the RBI in making productive use of the bounty of foreign exchange reserves during this phase of 2000-03 is writ large on the liberalisation of the exchange control regime. The liberalisation went beyond the recommendations of the Tarapore Committee, which had advocated a gradualist approach.

For instance, in terms of permitting resident Indians to invest abroad, the Tarapore Committee had recommended that this should be gradually liberalised. In contrast, today, resident Indians are permitted to invest abroad, without any financial ceilings; the only irritant is that exchange control specifies permissible avenues of investment such as multinational corporations which are listed in the stock market and so on.

The new regime is particularly generous to non-resident Indians (NRIs), who can now merrily repatriate proceeds of their assets sold in India. The ceilings on Indian corporates' investment abroad or in joint ventures are quite high and such liberalisation is not confined to capital account. Even in respect of current account, the permitted allowances for travel, business travel, education, and soon, are so liberal that one would have never thought that India would usher in such an over-generous regime. The gay abandon with which the RBI has gone on liberalising outflow of foreign reserves gives an impression that the central bank is embarrassed by the surge in reserves.

The RBI is almost apologetic about the unusually high level of reserves, as is reflected in the following statement in a recent publication: "The sharp increase in the reserves in the recent period have raised issues about the costs and benefits of reserves, the financial cost of additional reserve accretion is estimated to be low. These costs are likely to be more than offset by the return on additional reserves. Furthermore, high reserves have provided important benefits in the form of precautionary lines of defence against under seen external shocks, the welfare gains from smoothing domestic consumption and investment, and the more visible benefits of ensuring financial stability despite an unsatisfactory international environment."

Although the RBI has pontificated extensively on the adequate level of reserves, it does not seem to have evolved quantitative guidelines about the desired level of reserves. If, say, $30 billion of reserves are adequate – roughly equivalent to six months imports – could the economy use the 'surplus' reserves of, say, $40 billion for productive purposes?

For instance, power is acting as a major constraint on industrial growth and can we import some power plants straightaway? This is the kind of issue which the RBI should address in the present context. It would then be able to draw up the modalities by which utilisation of part of reserves for productive purposes would be rendered feasible. Instead, the present panicky reaction of the RBI to somehow reduce the size of reserves would fritter away the valuable reserves. One is reminded of the frittering away by India of the huge sterling balances in the post-War period. Is history repeating itself?

In a capital-scarce economy like that of India, it is difficult to understand the rationale behind prodding resident Indians to invest abroad. The collapse of the UTI, the moribund capital market, the so-called soft interest rate regime, are acting as a depressant on the household sector's savings. What purpose are these measures, to promote investment abroad, supposed to serve?

As it is, the bulk of the country's foreign exchange reserves are invested in developed countries such as the US, the UK and Germany. Do we want to reinforce this feature of public investment by promoting resident Indians also to invest abroad? Such efforts would be counter-productive. Thus, the basic approach to liberalise further the capital account convertibility is out-dated, flawed and premature.

Out-dated because the policy-makers who are adept in mimicking IMF/World Bank theology are yet to realise that the theology itself has changed. The IMF now sings a different tune.

Flawed because even empirical experience does not provide enough evidence to show that capital account openness necessarily results in large increases in capital inflows in developing countries.

On the other hand, the dangers to which it exposes developing countries are real, as emphasised by the *Economist*. Premature because the sort of pre-conditions set out by the Tarapore Committee are not fulfilled even today. The profligacy in the use of reserves, which is reflected in the current liberalisation of the exchange control regime, is unwarranted. The real challenge would be to facilitate the absorption of 'surplus' forex reserves by the economy, so that it leads to higher growth. Policy-makers would do well to address this question, rather than imitating outdated IMF prescriptions.

The Hindu Business Line, May 29, 2003.

V

Crisis of Capitalism

22

Crisis in American Capitalism

Lesson for India

Is American capitalism crumbling? Recent revelations of corporate crookedness and accounting scandals have shaken the very foundations of the American capitalist model. Corporate America's fall from grace has been sudden and complete.

The Enron, WorldCom and Xerox exposures have unveiled the darker side of western style capitalism where, in the quest for short-term gains, wrongdoings are often over-looked.

The financial fallout of WorldCom, for instance, is staggering. Its shareholders, once the owners of a $120-billion company, are now left with virtually nothing. Banks and bondholders have $41 billion in loans to WorldCom. A large chunk of this is unlikely to be repaid.

The collapse of Andersen, one of the big five accounting firms has, in the wake of the Enron scandal, added a new dimension to the systemic infirmities. This 'corporate-accounting firm-capital market' nexus has perhaps proved to be the last straw for the American capitalist system.

Corporate entities often fix a target price for their shares, and these are achieved with the help of obliging accounting firms that dress up the accounts so as to generate the required price-earnings ratio. Fudging of accounts seems to have evolved into a fine art. The depth of degradation to which unbridled corporate greed can lead has become all too obvious. These developments cannot be dismissed, as some apologists of American capitalism are doing, as isolated incidents. They are systemic.

According to Prof Lester C. Thurow of the Sloan School of Management at MIT, "The Enrons and WorldComs are not abnormalities in a 'basically sound system'. Scandals are endemic to capitalism."

That this point has been recognised by the US Government is clear from the fact that a crackdown on corporate crooks is now on top of the legislative agenda.

The US President, Mr. George Bush, has stated thus: "As part of the crack-down I support the creation of a strong independent board that will provide effective oversight of the accounting profession. This board would have the ability to monitor, investigate, and enforce high ethical principles by punishing individual offenders." But as Prof Thurow emphasises: "New laws and regulations adopted in the aftermath of scandal are almost always useless in preventing future wrongdoing, especially in financial matters. The last great wave of regulatory law making, designed to prevent systemic fraud and abuse among savings and loans in the 1980s proved largely irrelevant to preventing systemic fraud and abuse among accounting firms today."

The upheavals in the corporate world have had a dramatic impact on the capital market. On July 15, the Dow Jones individual index fell by 342 points to 8,332, the fifth triple-digit fall in six sessions. The NASDAQ composite index hit its lowest level since 1997 losing 56 points to touch 1,317. Corporate accounting scandals have made investors mistrustful of earnings reports and outlook studies. The US Ambassador to the Asian Development Bank and, ironically, an organiser of the Asia Corporate Governance Association, Ms Linda Tsao Yang, admits thus: "I have been a student of capital markets for 40 years.... and in that period, I have never seen the collapse of faith in the American Corporations that I see today," (*International Herald Tribune*, July 8, 2002).

In fact, there is more to it than the current wave of corporate and accounting scandals. The systemic infirmity of American capitalism is that the small investor is always at a disadvantage. Prof Thurow cautions the small investor: "The first and best solution is to warn all small investors that the game is rigged. No individual investor, no matter how well informed, can play on the same level as the major institutional investors. Wall Street firms and corporate executives receive more accurate information more quickly... The major players talk all the time, and very little of what they learn becomes known to the general public." In such crises, therefore, it is the small investor who suffers most.

Although the discovery of the fact that American capitalism is not infallible may not be as devastating as the collapse of communism in the Soviet Union, it does raise serious doubts about the desirability of economies such as India trying to replicate the American model. The experience has been particularly humbling for market theologists, including the IMF and the World Bank, who advocate that the US should be the standard setter as regards the capital market, accounting norms, corporate governance and the financial system as a whole. The current developments have, probably, made the architects of the global economy indulge in some rethinking.

Are there any lessons for India from this crisis in American capitalism? To start with, the policy-makers must reassess the reforms initiated in the 1990s with regard to the capital market, mutual funds and commercial banks. At the heart of the reforms has been the obsession to develop the capital market at the cost of other segments of the financial sector. Even today, promoting the equity cult seems to be the *mantra* of financial policy. Development banks such as the IDBI were de-emphasised and allowed to decay. Commercial banks were discriminated against *vis-à-vis* mutual funds. Artificial props such as fiscal incentives were given to boost equity investment. Several measures to attract foreign institutional investors (FIIs) into portfolio investment were taken. These efforts have, however, proved to be a failure.

Today, the capital market is moribund, mobilising in the past three years a mere Rs. 5,000 to 6,000 crore annually. It has become a breeding ground for financial scams. In contrast, the private placement market has witnessed dramatic growth, raising, on an average, Rs. 60,000 crore a year. The equity cult, in India, is not well-entrenched. Unlike in the industrial countries, the household sector is the predominant saver accounting for the bulk of total financial savings. And commercial banks have historically claimed the large slice of household sector savings.

It was rather thoughtless on the part of policy-makers to have ignored this historical link and attempt to divert savings away from commercial banks to mutual funds by discriminating against banks through fiscal measures.

Fortunately though, this discrimination ended in 2002-03. But enough damage has been done to the mobilisation efforts of commercial banks. The RBI, on its part, was irrational in prodding public sector banks (PSBs) to involve themselves increasingly, both directly and indirectly, in the capital market.

In fact, commercial banks have traditionally extended long-term credit to medium-sized industries. Thus, the best course would have been to allow banks to grow on their preferred lines rather than introduce distortions with a view to promoting the capital market.

Similarly, the IDBI has played a critical role in promoting growth of industries. Many of the medium-sized industrial houses owe their growth to IDBI assistance. There was no reason for the policy-makers to have de-emphasised IDBI's role, by withdrawing, among other concessions, RBI assistance. Today, the IDBI is not in the pink of its health.

Even in the tiger economies, development banks have played a crucial role in industrial growth. Reviving the IDBI and making it vibrant must, therefore, be given consideration.

Small savings form a significant component of household sector savings. Unfortunately, following the Reddy Committee recommendations, interest rates on small savings have been reduced drastically. The revised rates are not attractive and will affect savings growth as a whole.

If American capitalism has any lessons for India, it is with regard to the capital market, which has been given undue emphasis. Considering India's socio-economic milieu, alternative routes to promoting industries and encouraging banks to extend long-term credit to industries must be looked at.

In the zest to develop the capital market, several distortions have crept in. Banks must not be discriminated against and goaded to increasingly involve themselves in the capital market.

Small savings must be encouraged, by even offering higher interest rates so that higher levels of savings can be sustained.

Let the capital market develop on its own, not by artificial props and at the cost of other segments of the financial sector.

The Hindu Business Line, August 22, 2002.

23

Systemic Approach to Privatisation

The floundering disinvestment programme has brought to the centre stage a whole range of issues relating to privatisation and management of the economy.

For all the talk of going ahead with disinvestment, uncertainty surrounds the government's getting out of shipping, aluminium and fertiliser majors. The anti-disinvestment faction has become so vocal that the Prime Minister himself was compelled to reaffirm that this postponement does not indicate a U-turn on the sell-offs, and that the Government stands by its earlier commitment. But the NALCO episode seems to be turning this on its head.

Two related developments also need to be discussed in this context. On September 19, Standard & Poor's downgraded rupee-denominated government debt from BBB+ to BB+. The rating agency cited the government's "growing rupee debt burden" and "its inability to staunch the financial weakening of the public sector". Second, this loss of investment grade status was reinforced by the fact that India has dropped out of A.T. Kearney's list of the top 10 foreign direct investment destinations. It now stands at a dismal 15th position.

These two developments added fuel to the disinvestment lobby, which in any case was arguing that if privatisation is postponed indefinitely, India would not be able to attract foreign investment. What about China, which does not have even the basic civil laws relating to property, etc., but which has been a resounding success in attracting huge foreign investments? Nor has China carried out financial sector reforms on the Western models, as India has done.

Some Indian management experts argue that the fiscal deficit in 2002-03 may rise to 6 per cent of GDP and, hence, the need to disinvest in many public sector enterprises, so that the proceeds could be used to reduce the fiscal deficit. This only demonstrates how poorly equipped they are to deal with macro management of the economy.

Fiscal profligacy *per se* needs to be condemned, of course. But the suggestion that such profligacy be balanced using the proceeds of privatisation needs to be condemned severely. This is like selling the family silver to buy groceries. Thus, some mythology is woven around the imperatives of privatisation as if the latter is an end-objective of development in itself.

Would privatisation in a particular segment lead to greater efficiency in the use of resources and promote faster GDP growth? This is the question we ought to pose and not to what extent the fiscal deficit would fall by selling some public sector undertakings (PSUs). What you do with the proceeds of privatisation is as important as why you need to privatise a particular unit or segment of the public sector. The real economic issues are obfuscated because of the emotional and political undertones the debate has acquired. What we need is a systemic approach to privatisation.

Private sector, *per se,* particularly the private corporate sector, is no paragon of virtue, as some Indian advocates of privatisation seem to be arguing. The current crisis in American capitalism is ample proof of this statement. The recent revelations of corporate and accounting scandals have shaken the very foundations of the American capitalist model, which the present-day policy-makers appear keen to replicate in India.

Corporate American's fall from grace has been sudden and complete. The Enron, WorldCom and Xerox exposures, coupled with the collapse of Andersen, one of the world's big five accounting firms, have unveiled the darker side of American-style capitalism. A doctrinaire approach to privatisation, which seems to be the current fashion, is no more justifiable than a doctrinaire approach to state enterprises.

Many public sector enterprises in India may be inefficient and loss-making, but that does not automatically establish the superiority of private sector. We have had our own Enrons and WorldComs, though on a smaller scale.

All this goes to show that a rational and systemic approach to privatisation is warranted. Three dimensions of such an approach could be briefly spelt out:

- utilisation of the proceeds of privatisation;
- choice of public sector units for privatisation; and
- reform of the public sector enterprises management.

All the proceeds of sell-offs of public sector units must be pooled and put into a "consolidated sinking fund", as proposed by the Reserve Bank of India (RBI) in 1995-96. This fund should be earmarked for redemption of government debt. While everyone seems concerned about the mounting public debt, precious little is being done to reduce it.

Using these funds to reduce the fiscal deficit is counterproductive. As mentioned above, you cannot sell the family silver to buy groceries.

This is tantamount to camouflaging the real size of the fiscal deficit. Reducing the fiscal deficit is a formidable problem that needs to be tackled head on and transparently. Not undertaking any privatisation is preferable to using its proceeds for reducing fiscal deficit. Moreover, some broad ground rules should be formulated on the choice of public sector undertakings for privatisation, rather than proceeding in an *ad hoc* manner.

PSUs that are chronically loss-making must be sold first. This criteria is analogous to settlement of non-performing assets (NPAs) of commercial banks, on a once-for-all settlement basis. In any case, such loss-making PSUs are some sort of fiscal termites, and getting rid of them would stem the fiscal rot. Again, there is another genre of fiscal termites, namely, enterprises that are prevented from functioning efficiently because of social and political compulsions. Power is one such segment. In Maharashtra, as the Godbole Committee brought out, one-third of the power generated and distributed is not "billed" — the so-called leakage. This is the case with many State electricity boards. This segment is an ideal candidate for privatisation.

Finally, reform of the PSUs should be undertaken simultaneously with privatisation. Economic reforms should not be equated with privatisation alone.

If some PSUs have become sick it may be because of political and bureaucratic meddling.

For instance, IDBI was at one point of time an ideal institution — competent viable and vibrant. Why has it become sick today, requiring blood transfusion from the Government? Would autonomy and professional management help restore vibrancy in all such cases?

Basically, efficiency is ownership-neutral. Hence, if there are some PSUs which are profit-making and offering excellent services, there is no reason why these should be privatised. Not, surely, on the grounds that America does not have such PSUs.

Then, again, there are other macroeconomic factors that affect the flow of foreign investment.

For instance, A.T. Kearney advances the following reason for downgrading India as a foreign direct investment destination. "The simmering conflict with Pakistan over Jammu and Kashmir undoubtedly deters foreign investors, while Budget deficits and poor infrastructure have imposed further constraints."

In any case, foreign investment flows have stagnated at around $5,000 million for the last three years.

Aggregate foreign investment, including direct investment and portfolio investment, rose to $5,925 million in 2001-02, from $5,099 million the previous year. In 1999-00 the figure was $5,181 million. In fact, the RBI patted itself on the back by stating that the level of foreign investment in 2001-02 is "demonstrative of growing global investors confidence in the Indian economy."

Interestingly, there was actually a reduction in portfolio investment flows from $2,760 million in 2000-01 to $2,021 million in 2001-02.

Both foreign institutional investment (FII) inflows and amounts raised through the GDR/ADR route were lower than in the previous year.

It is thus obvious whether India is moving faster towards privatisation or slowing down its pace has not much to do with foreign investment inflows. This myth needs to be exploded.

This brings us to the policy-makers' obsessive concern with developing the capital market. With all the rhetoric about the promotion of capital market, resources raised through the primary market have stagnated at a dismal Rs. 7,000 crore during the last two years.

This is not surprising because it seems to be part of the global phenomenon.

The Economist of London calls the recent depression in the American capital market "the bursting of the biggest financial bubble in American history.

During the bubble years, decisions across the whole economy about investment borrowing and saving were distorted by unrealistic expectations about future profits and share prices and a belief that the business cycle was dead."

Against this broader background, some Indian experts' plea for faster privatisation with the ostensible objectives of attracting larger foreign investment flows and of developing the Indian capital market sounds hollow.

Let us proceed with privatisation, by all means, but unclouded by all the myth built around it by vested interests and by adopting a systemic approach based on rational grounds.

Larger public investments in infrastructure, reviving development banks such as the IDBI and reform of PSUs — all these appear to be more sensible policies than propitiation of foreign investment.

The Hindu Business Line, November 8, 2002.

24

Good Governance: Form and Substance

The subject of corporate governance has been brought on the centre-stage of macroeconomic management during the last decade or so. In the UK, four hefty reports, beginning with the Cadbury Report, in 1992, which defined the role of independent directors on the board of a company, were produced. The latest is the one by Derek Higgs, a banker, on the role of non-executives.

In the US, the Enron scam symbolised the crisis in American capitalism and the post-Enron fire and brimstone have brought in several far-reaching changes which extend beyond conventional corporate governance. The nexus between corporates, auditors and the capital market revealed in the Enron, WorldCom and Anderson scandals has added a new dimension to corporate governance issues. The recent Sarbanes-Oxley Act fixes new reporting standards for US auditors and top managements and prescribes stiff penalties if they fail to meet them.

Indian policy-makers of the liberalisation era are by now well-known as great imitators of the Western models, irrespective of their relevance to Indian-specific socio-economic milieu. This is particularly true of financial sector reforms. No wonder if this flurry of activity in the area of corporate governance has influenced Indian policy-makers and now we have our own quota of reports. The Kumar-Mangalam Birla Committee, set up by the Securities and Exchange Board of India (SEBI), submitted its Report in 1999.

The Naresh Chandra Committee Report (2003) carried forward the recommendations of the Birla Committee. Again, the committee on corporate governance was constituted by SEBI, under the chairmanship of Mr. N.R. Narayana Murthy to evaluate the adequacy of the existing corporate governance practices and to suggest how best to further improve them.

The Committee submitted its final report in 2003. Shorn of rhetorics, the essence of these recommendations are: all companies of a certain size, say, with a paid-up capital of Rs. 10 crore should have half the total number of its board numbers as independent directors; and the audit committees of all such companies should comprise only independent directors. There should be accountability and transparency and improved disclosers relating to compensation paid to non-executive directors.

It is hoped that these recommendations, which codify certain standards of good governance, when implemented through SEBI's regulatory framework, will strengthen existing governance practices and also provide a strong incentive to avoid corporate failures.

Through these efforts the mechanics of corporate governance, as understood by the western countries, is being mimicked, without considering the social milieu under which good corporate governance can be nurtured. Limiting the age of directors to 75, as the Indian company law is seeking to do, or insisting that nobody should chair more than one big company, as recommended by Derek Higgs, are merely gimmicks which will simply not work. No regulatory framework, however stringent, would be able to tame rogue corporates. According to Prof. Lester C. Thurow of the Sloan School of Management, MIT: "The Enrons and WorldComs are not abnormalities in a basically sound system. Scandals are endemic to capitalism."

"One of the oddities of corporate governance," writes *The Economist*, "is that what looks like a sound structure in one country is anathema to another." Citing three different structures, in Germany with two boards, one to supervise and one to manage, in the UK with unitary boards, and in the US with only non-executives on the board apart from the chief executive, to maximise the number of supposedly independent voices; *The Economist* comes to the conclusion: "But, all three countries have their share of corporate scandals, suggesting that good governance is driven more by the climate of acceptable behaviour than by board structure." (January 25-31). How independent is an independent director? It is only natural that the management of a company would prefer to choose an amenable independent" to be on board. The really independent would, thus, never have a chance to be on the board. That brings us to crux of the problem: contemporary Indian society is afflicted by moral pollution which is not confined to the corporate sector but is all pervasive. In such a climate, mere gimmicks of reforming the corporate sector would not automatically guarantee good governance. What is required is the evolution of a culture of social conscience and this is the task, which needs to be addressed by social scientists.

The litany of instances of moral pollution is long. There were two major scams of the capital market, one in 1992 and another in 2001. In the later, even the cooperative sector, which is supposed to have its own philosophy, was also involved. Several non-banking financial companies, which had witnessed mushroom growth initially, disappeared. The rapacious activities of the so-called "blade companies" in Kerala, the teak wood plantation schemes and time-sharing travel companies, are all well-documented.

The collapse of the UTI was the mother of all betrayals of the small investors, particularly because in its management both the Government of India and Reserve Bank of India (RBI) were involved. To what extent were these happenings attributed to bad corporate governance and other factors? Viewed in this context, one can begin to appreciate the difference between form and substance.

Going beyond the corporate sector, take the case of electricity boards. In one of them, one-third of the total power distributed was not 'billed' and treated as transmission and distribution loss. It would be paradoxical to talk of good governance in such a situation. The recruitment scandals in the case of some state public service commissions have exposed how corruption can penetrate the citadels of probity.

In the field of education, there are scandals of marks fixing and promotion of teachers on consideration other than merit. In the sphere of public health care, there are primary health centres in the villages and paramedics are appointed. But some of these centres are rarely open for actual treatment.

In such a climate of pervasive moral pollution, how does one go about improving corporate governance. Certainly not by SEBI's regulatory framework alone.

The roots of corporates accountability stem from the fact that corporates gather capital from a large number of investors. When an investor invests money in a corporation, he expects the board and the management to act as trustees and ensure the safety of the capital and a fair rate of return.

As the Narayana Murthy Committee Report puts it: "Corporate governance is the acceptance by management of the inalienable rights of shareholders as the true owners of the corporation and of their own role as trustees on behalf of the shareholders. It is about commitment to values, about ethical business conduct and about making a distinction between personal and corporate funds in the management of the company." Inculcating these values among all directors, whether independent or not, involves raising the social conscience – about the macro environment in which a company operates, the abject poverty, disease and illiteracy that surround us.

Some management experts have argued that the corporates must be judged by the wealth that they create. Why judge them by charities they offer to different stakeholders in society? It is not really a question of charity but a sense of social responsibility.

The concept of "shared growth" has now become part of the accepted development philosophy. Only such shared growth can ensure the sustainability of development. To take a concrete case, the chief executive officer of a multinational claims total emoluments of, say, Rs. 2 crore per year. Is this justified in the Indian situation where even the RBI Governor may earn only Rs. 6 lakh or so per year?

Nobody would argue that the responsibilities of RBI Governor are any less onerous than the CEO of the multinational. It is not only the quantum of wealth created by a corporate that is important. How this wealth is created and how is it finally disbursed are also equally important. Some of the stories about the enormous amounts of emoluments and perks that Enron executives were entitled to are enlightening in this context.

Good governance is required not only in the case of big corporates in the private sector; small enterprises, public sector undertakings, educational institutions and universities, public health care, banks and financial institutions need to be injected with a large dose of good governance. And this task cannot be achieved by merely importing forms or models from Western countries. Social conscience must be aroused among all sections of the population, through education, training and publicity.

Transparency in the conduct of business can be ensured only through this process. The ultimate accountability of a CEO or a public figure is to the society at large and not only to shareholders or stakeholders and evolving a society of conscience keepers should be our objective. Citadels of probity should be built in all segments of the economy or society and these would induce others to emulate. This is the substance of good governance.

The Hindu Business Line, July 8, 2003.

VI

Fiscal Policies

25

Kelkar Proposals

An Accountant's Approach to Tax Reforms

The Kelkar Committee on Direct Taxes – called the Task Force on Direct Taxes – like the Reddy committee on small savings which submitted its report earlier – lacks a macroeconomic perspective. The Kelkar Committee report emphasises that "the recommendations of the report are embedded in a forward-looking approach to taxation by imparting a sector-neutral flavour".

Furthermore, the recommendations "pertaining to direct tax codes are congruent with generally-accepted principles of taxation. The three principles relate to efficiency (minimising distortions in resource allocation), equity (progressiveness of effective tax rates), and effectiveness (of tax administration)".

If one takes an analytical view of the impact of the totality of these recommendations, it becomes clear that both equity and sector neutrality would be sacrificed, if these recommendations are implemented. The core recommendations are overwhelmingly biased in favour of the dividend-seeking class and against small-savers – which includes salary earners and retirees. The economic support to the major recommendations is extremely weak, the underlying logic flawed and the Committee seems to be oblivious of the net costs and benefits of implementing each of these measures. The tax incentives provided in the present system mean so much revenue foregone and hence nullify the exemptions.

This is an accountant's approach to tax reform and not an economist's. Fiscal policy involves much more than merely arithmetically balancing income and expenditure. The small savers as a class are already hurt by the low interest rate regime, reduction of interest rates on certain savings instruments following the recommendations of the Reddy Committee, and the collapse of the UTI.

On top of these, the Kelkar Committee recommends the elimination of the following tax incentives for savings : tax rebate schemes under Section 88 for savings; the rebate under Section 88B for senior citizens; the income-based reduction under Section 80L for interest income and dividends; and the exemption under Section 10 in respect of interest income from bonds, securities etc.

If these recommendations are accepted, they would hasten the not-so-decent burial of the small-savers as a class. The impact would be highly inequitable among cross-sections of the population and, perhaps, an alienation of the middle-class, which lends both political and economic stability to the society.

The Committee states: "First, there is hardly any evidence to prove that tax incentives have, *per se*, increased investment or saving – for which these incentives were devised." One has to look at the incentives in a broader context of raising the effective rate of return on small-savings and, as a consequence, make these savings instruments more attractive.

The Reddy Committee itself provides some evidence to substantiate this point. For instance, the share of small savings as a percentage of net financial savings of the household sector rose from 7.9 per cent in 1996-97 to 13.8 per cent in 1998-99. In fact, in the 1990s, the gross collections from these schemes grew at a phenomenal rate of 17 per cent per annum, compared to bank deposits growth of 13 per cent.

Even macro studies, which have examined the phenomenon of how a low-saving Indian economy of, say, 5 or 7 per cent of GDP in the 1950s graduated into a high-saving economy of, say, 25 per cent of GDP in the late 1970s, have pointed out that beyond a threshold, savings are sensitive to rate of interest or returns. One would wish the Committee had made an in depth study of this issue, rather than abruptly dismissing it as irrelevant.

The recommendations of the Kelkar Committee aimed at developing the capital market are startling in contrast to those relating to tax incentives provided to promote savings. First, dividends received from Indian companies would be fully exempt from tax. Second, long-term capital gains on equity would be fully exempt. Third, in addition to exemption of dividend from taxation in the hands of shareholders, there will be also no tax on distribution of dividends by a company. Fourth, the minimum alternate tax on corporates under Section 115 JB is also eliminated. One begins to wonder whether this tax holiday phobia is inspired by the IMF/World Bank mythology.

What is the empirical evidence to prove that these extremely liberal measures would result in a healthy development of the capital market?

Perhaps, the Committee was wise in not raising the issue because efforts to develop the capital market provide an excellent example of heroic failure. All the artificial props given by the Government and the Reserve Bank of India to boost the capital market since the liberalisation phase of 1990s, have resulted in the emergence of a moribund capital market today. Throwing open the portfolio investment to foreign institutional investors (FIIs), exempting dividends from tax, RBI prodding public sector banks to involve themselves increasingly both directly and indirectly in the stock market, institutional support through establishment of SEBI, have proved of no avail.

In the early 1990s it was possible to raise capital through new issues on the stock market to the extent of Rs. 10,000 crore a year and the expectation was that this could be raised to some Rs. 50,000 crore a year in the late 1990s or early 2000s. Unfortunately, the average capital raised during the last three years was hardly in the region of Rs. 7,000 crore.

This is not all. The path to the development of the capital market in the 1990s is strewn with corpses. It is not without significance that the stock market has been a breeding ground of major scams of the financial sector in recent years. Given this track record of the capital market, it would be self-destructive for the fiscal policy to focus its concessions exclusively on the capital market, at the cost of other segments of the financial system.

There are alternatives to the capital market which can be developed. The IDBI and the ICICI can be revitalised. More recently, the RBI has rightly asked public sector banks to involve themselves increasingly in extending medium and long-term finance to projects.

We should also encourage internal generation of resources by the corporate sector – a source which is prominent in the developed countries. Against this broader perspective, it is necessary that small savings, bank deposits and dividends enjoy a level-playing field in respect of fiscal incentives. This would ensure 'equity' amongst the cross-section of the population.

The innocence of the Kelkar Committee of the macro ramifications of fiscal measures is reflected in another important recommendation on housing. The deduction of mortgage interest in respect of loans for acquiring owner-occupied dwellings should be phased out by 2006-07. This is unfortunate because housing activity is the best means for promoting saving and capital formation. Housing is not only a labour-intensive industry but also has forward and backward linkages. Even in the developed countries, housing is promoted through fiscal and financial concessions.

Overall, one does not have to be a socialist to assert that any system designed to permit dividend – income of, say, Rs. 1 crore – to go tax-free but taxes interest income of a middle-class saver with a bank deposit of, say, Rs. 1 lakh. But this is essentially what the Kelkar Committee has set out to advocate.

The panel insists that the various recommendations relating to personal income-tax in this report are inter-woven and, therefore, indivisible. The recommendations must be seen as a package and piecemeal implementation should be avoided at all cost.

This article clearly demonstrates that implementation of the totality of its recommendations would be both economically and politically suicidal. Hence, respecting the desire of the Committee, its recommendations should be rejected *in toto*. Of course, its recommendations relating to modernisation of tax administration are very well-thought out and, hence, should be implemented straightway.

The Hindu Business Line, November 22, 2003.

26

Kelkar Panel Final Report

Fraught with Elitist Bias

The Kelkar Task Force seems to be exulting over the massive response to its original proposals on direct tax reforms – it is said to have received 1,500 e-mails, 100 memoranda, over 200 articles and much feedback through discussions with trade and industry. The Task Force, however, has not classified the responses into those which broadly support the proposals and those which do not.

The core recommendations, over-whelmingly biased in favour of dividend earners and the corporate elite, have evoked massive protests. But these have apparently failed to influence the Task Force, because the revised proposals, too, have remained essentially the same. The logic of the Task Force seems to be to target the classes which do not count, and pamper those which do – the more vocal and those having clout, that is. If the revised proposals are accepted *in toto*, a sizeable transfer of income from the middle class – comprising salary earners, small savers and retirees – to the upper income groups will take place. Perhaps, this is what the market theology recommends. In any case, the income-tax system would become highly regressive.

What is more, if the objective of the revised proposals is to promote the capital market, empirical evidence shows that this will not be achieved. Unlike in developed countries such as the US or the UK, household sector savings contribute the core of India's savings, built up assiduously since the latter half of the 1970s and, thereby, helping turn the economy into a high savings one. The revised proposals would deliver a deathblow to the savings culture. The only consolation is that the panel has responded to the criticism on the elimination of concessions to housing finance and senior citizens.

The most disturbing feature of the recommendations is the elimination of all tax concessions that promote small savings.

According to the report, the tax incentives for savings under Sections 88, 801, 10(15) (1), 10(15)(iib), 10(15)(iic), 10(15)(iid), 10(15)(iv)(h) and 10(15)(iv)(i) of the Income-Tax Act must all be eliminated with immediate effect and not through a sunset clause.

The tax incentives had, of late, resulted in a phenomenal growth in small savings. But if the concessions are withdrawn, small savings are bound to dry up.

Contrast this with the corporate scene if the revised proposals are implemented. The tax rate for both domestic and foreign companies would be lower, at 30 per cent and 35 per cent respectively. Also, there will be no tax on dividends distributed by a company; the dividends would be exempt in the hands of shareholders as well. Again, long-term capital gains on listed equity would be exempted. The minimum alternate tax (MAT), under Section 115 JB, would be eliminated.

The contrast is quite clear. On the one hand, the Government is snatching a sizeable amount from what can be broadly categorised as the small-savers class, by eliminating the tax incentives and, on the other, it is forgoing revenues from the corporate sector by reducing the tax rate and abolishing dividend tax. According to the Task Force, "Overall, the recommendations are revenue neutral at the existing level of compliance."

The panel's tax strategy, as reflected in the revised proposals, lends itself to the interpretation that small savers would in a way subsidise the corporate sector.

What is the rationale for this 'soft' approach to the corporate sector? Rather than explaining the rationale, if any, the revised report obfuscates the issue: "A corporate entity should be viewed as a 'conduit' and, therefore, the need for integration of corporate tax and personal income-tax. Given the pros and cons of the various full/partial integration methods, the Task Force recommends the adoption of this method of full integration of corporation and personal income-tax, whereby a tax at the corporate level is levied at the same rate as the maximum rate of personal income-tax and all dividends and capital gains is exempted from tax in the hands of shareholders. Accordingly, the Task Force recommends a corporate tax rate of 30 per cent for domestic companies, being the top marginal rate for personal income-tax, and exempt from tax all dividends and long-term capital gains from listed equity. This method would not undermine any equity since most direct equity investors in the companies in India are likely to be taxed at the top marginal rate of personal income-tax."

One may ask how dividend income is different from 'other income'. After all income is income, whether derived from dividend on equity investment or interest from bank deposits. Those who receive interest income could as well argue that their bank has already paid tax on income and, therefore, the interest income needs to be exempted from income-tax.

When the Finance Ministry is concerned about the declining tax-GDP ratio and the increasing fiscal deficit, there is no reason why corporate tax should be reduced or dividend tax abolished. Would these tax reforms boost the capital market? The track record of the Indian capital market shows that they will not. Since liberalisation measures were introduced in the early 1990s, policy-makers appear to be obsessed with the development of the capital market – perhaps at the behest of the IMF and the World Bank. Throwing open portfolio investments to foreign institutional investors (FIIs), prodding public sector banks to involve themselves increasingly, both directly and indirectly, in the capital market, exempting dividend incomes and incomes from mutual funds from tax have been some of the major policy initiatives. But what has been the net result?

In the early 1990s, the capital raised from new issues averaged around Rs. 10,000 crore a year. The expectation was that with all the props, it would be possible to raise about Rs. 50,000 crore a year by end-1990s. In fact, the annual average of capital raised through new issues was around only Rs. 7,000 crore in the past three years. It is time the policy-makers grew out the obsession of developing the capital market. The world over, capital markets have ceased to be the barometer of economic activity. Nor does corporate growth depend much on the capital market. Even in developed countries the funds raised through the capital market account for hardly 20 per cent of the total capital formation of the corporate sector.

However, two modifications that the panel has made deserve special mention. Originally, the panel had recommended that the ceiling on mortgage interest that is deductible be reduced from Rs. 1,50,000 to a mere Rs. 50,000. In the revised version, it has softened the blow, recommending a 2 per cent interest rate subsidy on all housing loans below Rs. 5 lakh, which is to be granted by the Government through the National Housing Bank. This, though welcome, makes the whole business of housing loans messy, substituting rebates with exemptions and *vice versa*.

The second modification relates to senior citizens. The original proposal had recommended the elimination of the Rs. 15,000 tax rebate available to senior citizens. The revised version raises the exemption limit for senior citizens to Rs. 1,50,000 against the Rs. 1,00,000 for the general category of taxpayers. The tax rebate for senior citizens is, thus, restored.

Apart from the nitty-gritty of individual tax changes, the overall strategy of tax proposals envisages the transfer of a sizeable chunk of income, as it were, from the lower- and middle-income groups to the corporate sector and the dividend earning upper-income group, by snatching away tax concessions from the former and facilitating the flow of funds so saved to latter through new tax concessions. This is a dangerous strategy.

First, it eliminates the lower- and middle-income groups from participating in the growth process. And, second, it would destroy the savings culture of the household sector, which has been responsible for raising and sustaining the high savings rate of the Indian economy.

The Hindu Business Line, January 23, 2003.

27

Rediscovering the Priorities

The tragedy of India's liberalisation process in the 1990s was that the policy-makers began to follow IMF/World Bank recommendations, such as cutting down the fiscal deficit, eliminating all subsidies – including those for food, liberalising imports, evolving a market-determined exchange rate and developing the capital market, blindly.

Intrinsically, there was nothing wrong with the recommendations, but what happened was that policy-makers focussed only on these areas and ignored other pressing issues, such as poverty reduction, elimination of hunger, development of agriculture, employment generation – particularly in the rural areas, and improving the quality of life. The policy-makers exulted in the GDP growth of more than 6 per cent in 1998-99 and 1999-2000. But this was jobless growth. With a view to reducing the food subsidy, the foodgrains prices distributed through fair price shops were raised, and also access to the public distribution system narrowed. The cumulative result of these policies was the more than 60 million tonnes of so-called surplus foodgrains. In a country which has the largest number of underfed and under-nourished people, this mountain of foodgrains stands as a monument of its misconceived policies.

Hence, it was left to the Finance Minister, Mr. Jaswant Singh, to rediscover the right priorities. "This Budget is about addressing the problem of poverty and lifetime concerns of our citizens, of giving a major boost to infrastructure and laying the foundations for balanced, accelerated growth of agriculture and industry, plus tax reform. I have tried to address the 'Panch Priorities' and I hope that after this year of drought our economy will respond favourably to the Budget package and demonstrate impressive growth in 2003-04," he said.

The Finance Minister is aware that the Budget deficit rose to 5.9 per cent of GDP in 2002-03, well above the estimates. But there were extenuating circumstances. GDP growth declined to 4.4 per cent from

5.6 per cent largely due to a decline in agricultural growth by nearly 12 per cent. Fortunately, the industry witnessed a remarkable recovery and recorded a 6 per cent growth, and this is expected to further improve in 2003-04. Despite the anticipated robust growth, the Budget deficit will still be fairly high at 5.6 per cent of GDP. Despite fairly high levels of Budget deficits in the last couple of years, it has been possible to contain inflation at well below 4 per cent. Has the conventional output-money-price relationship broken down after all? In any case, with plentiful supply of wage goods, mainly foodgrains, and a more than comfortable level of forex reserves, it should be possible to contain inflation. It is time we outgrew the Budget deficit obsession and got on with development. That seems to be the refrain of the Finance Minister whose speech went beyond the conventional arithmetic idioms.

Perhaps for the first time, a bold attempt has been made to attack poverty directly through the utilisation of surplus foodgrains. The Antyodaya Anna Yojana will be expanded to cover an additional 50 lakh families in 2003-04. Thus, more than a quarter of the families below the poverty line (BPL) will be covered in 2003-04. This involves an expenditure of Rs. 507 crore. It may not be possible to substantially reduce poverty levels, but it is certainly possible to eliminate hunger immediately.

One hopes that the Prime Minister goes further and attacks hunger directly. For instance, he can institute a "grain loan facility" under which the Food Corporation of India (FCI) will provide foodgrains on loan to institutions such as the Khadi and Village Industries Commission (KVIC) and State village industries boards. The recipient institutions can generate additional employment in the decentralised sector, thereby enabling the rural unemployed to sustain themselves. In fact, 2003-04 can be devoted to fulfil the Finance Minister's assurance of "*Garib Ke Pet Me Dana*". In any case the re-ordering of priorities was indeed overdue.

Also relevant in this context are the whole range of programmes relating to infrastructure, agricultural and rural development. Many of these are labour-intensive and will go a long way towards employment expansion. Demand generated by enhanced public investments in infrastructure, the Finance Minister emphasises, has been a key stimulant for the current industrial recovery. It may be recalled that in

October 1998, the Prime Minister launched the National Highway Development Project (NHDP), one of the most ambitious highway projects in the world providing strong backward linkages to steel and cement industries. The Budget for 2003-04 adds 48 new road projects at a cost of Rs. 40,000 crore, with a total length of 10,000 km.

Again, there is the rural roads programme under the Pradhan Mantri Gram Sadak Yojana for which some Rs. 2,325 crore has been allocated. In respect of agriculture, a new central sector scheme on hi-tech horticulture and precision farming will be introduced this year.

In the area of rural credit, the most important development is the lowering of rural lending rates. All along the process of financial sector reforms, the rural sector was discriminated against. While a highly rated corporate entity could access bank credit at, say, 7 to 8 per cent, the small farmer continued to pay 12 per cent. The benefits of the low interest rate regime, thus, did not percolate to the rural sector. The State Bank of India has announced that its lending rates to agriculture and small-scale industries will not be higher than 2 per cent above its prime lending rate (PLR). Other public sector banks are expected to follow. Thus, farmers and small scale industrialists will now be able to access bank credit at rates no higher than 2 per cent above the rates charged to the bank's best customer. Further, the Finance Minister has exhorted the States to boost the micro-credit programmes, especially the self-help group (SHG) commercial bank linked credit programmes. Thus, the access of the rural poor to bank credit will be enhanced and the cost of credit will be brought down.

Savings and Personal Income-Tax

The Finance Minister should be congratulated for rejecting many recommendations made by the Kelkar Committee on direct taxes. The recommendations relating to the abolition of tax concessions to small savings, housing loans, and to senior citizens have to be rejected. In respect of dividend income, the recommendation that dividends be exempted from tax at the hands of recipients has been accepted, but the tax on dividend distribution at the company level has been fixed at 12.5 per cent, rejecting the Kelkar task force recommendations.

The blow to small savings came in the form of a reduction of one percentage of interest payable on all small savings instruments, including the public provident fund (PPF). This was the unkindest cut. The RBI followed this up by announcing an interest cut on savings accounts from 4 per cent to 3.5 per cent. In India, unlike in the developed countries, the household sector is the main contributor to overall financial savings, and any measure which acts as a disincentive to the household sector savings may jeopardise the overall savings rate.

One wonders whether there is a hidden agenda in discriminating against bank deposits and small savings, and for investment in equity. This fiscal discrimination exempts dividends from income-tax but taxes income from bank deposits. The interest rates policy also discriminates against bank deposits. The low interest rate regime has already brought down interest rates on bank deposits to the lowest levels. The reduction in rates on small savings was, perhaps, made in the expectation that an asset reallocation in favour of investment in equity will take place. This is again a totally misconceived concept.

The obsessive concern to develop the capital market is part of the IMF/World Bank theology. The efforts of the Government of India and the RBI to develop the capital market during the last 10 to 12 years by giving artificial props have failed. In the early 1990s, capital raised through new issues averaged some Rs. 10,000 crore per year.

The expectation was that with the artificial props given to boost the market, this figure will rise to some Rs. 50,000 crore during the late 1990s. Unfortunately, the reality turned out to be different. The annual average of capital raised was only Rs. 7,000 crore in the last three years.

The policy-makers should realise that in the India specific situation, bank deposits resources mobilised through small savings and through the capital market are all equally important. Hence, it is necessary to provide a level-playing field to the three sources of savings. There is no need to pamper the dividends incomes.

While on the subject of savings, it is also necessary to refer to gold imports. The Budget reduced the Customs duty on imported gold to Rs. 100 per 10 grams from the present level of Rs. 250. Why? In fact our basic approach to gold imports during the liberalisation phase defies all logic.

What purpose on earth can such massive imports of gold serve? Liberalisation is all right within limits but a resource-scarce country such as India cannot afford to spend such massive amounts on import of gold.

Surely, WTO norms do not stipulate such unbridled liberalisation of gold imports. Even if one-half of the resources expended on gold imports are diverted to the capital market, it will boost it. This is an aspect of savings which warrants re-thinking.

The Hindu Business Line, March 13, 2003.

28

Fiscal Prudence

Centre Must Lead the Way

There has been considerable deterioration in State finances in recent years. For instance, the fiscal deficit of States rose from 3.3 per cent of GDP in 1990-91 to 4.6 per cent in 2001-02. The higher growth of revenue expenditure is largely responsible for this. The revenue deficit has nearly trebled from 0.9 per cent of GDP in 1990-91 to 2.6 per cent in 2001-02.

The large current revenue deficit is a deep-rooted structural problem common to both the Central and state governments. No wonder, therefore, that states are often tempted to utilise higher amounts of the Ways and Means Advances (WMA) and take overdrafts.

In October 2002, the RBI Governor, Dr. Bimal Jalan, constituted an Advisory Committee under the chairmanship of Mr. C. Ramachandran, former Secretary, Ministry of Finance, Government of India to review the normal WMA, special WMA and overdrafts to state governments. The Committee submitted its report in January, and the RBI decided to implement the major recommendations – with some modifications – from March.

Of course, streamlining state finances is a larger issue which is being looked into by Twelfth Finance Commission under the chairmanship of Dr. C. Rangarajan. Rationalising the WMA system can be regarded as an important step towards this. Fortunately, for the RBI, unlike the Centre, states do not have unlimited access to its resources. The RBI can stop payment to states when they cross the overdraft limits. But the Government must realise that fiscal profligacy at the Centre cannot co-exist with fiscal austerity at the state level. Overall, fiscal prudence should be the co-operative exercise of both the Centre and the states. In a federal system, the Centre must set an example for states to emulate.

Following the recommendations of the Ramachandran Committee, let us look at the reforms introduced by the RBI. Basically, the RBI provides WMA to states to help them tide over temporary mismatches in the cash flow of their receipts and payments. There are two types of WMA – normal and special. While normal WMA are clean advances, special WMA are secured advances provided against the pledge of government securities.

Any amount drawn by a state in excess of the stipulated WMA limit is called overdraft. Under the present overdraft regulations scheme, no state is allowed to run an overdraft with the RBI for more than 12 consecutive working days. In case a state remains in overdraft beyond the stipulated 12 days, the RBI and its agencies will "stop payment" in respect of that state.

This is the most effective way of preventing states from falling into the trap of fiscal profligacy. Similarly, if a state is in overdraft in excess of the 100 per cent of the stipulated WMA limit for more than five consecutive days, the RBI and its agencies will "stop payment". How one wishes that such checks applied to the Centre as well.

The main recommendations which have been accepted can be grouped under five categories: rationalisation of the formula for fixing the limits of WMA, higher rates of interest on drawals beyond 90 days, liberalisation of the special WMA scheme, a longer period for triggering stoppage of payment and a penal rate interest for overdrafts exceeding 100 per cent of the WMA limits.

The WMA limits will now be fixed on the basis of average revenue receipts of the preceding three years. So far, revenue receipts plus capital expenditure was the basis. The new formula is more rational because earlier the relevance of capital expenditure for the exercise was unclear.

The new formula is worked out in the basis of the average revenue receipts for three fiscal years 1999-2000 to 2001-02 and then the multiplication factor of 3.19 per cent is applied to this average. As per the new formula, the total normal WMA limits will work out to Rs. 7,170 crore compared to the present Rs. 6,035 crore. The minimum normal WMA limit remains unchanged at Rs. 50 crore. Thus, the new formula appears to have liberalised the facility.

Second, the rate of interest charged on the normal WMA will be the bank rate, that is, at 6.25 per cent at present for up to 90 days and one percentage point above the bank rate for thereafter. Third, the special WMA has been liberalised in terms of lower margin and interest rate. The special WMA will continue to be linked, as at present, to the States' investments in government securities.

For operating the limit of special WMA, the 5 per cent margin will be applied on the market value of securities, against the varying margin of 10 to 15 per cent now. Similarly, the interest rate will be 1 per cent below the bank rate. Since this facility is in the nature of secured advances, the liberalisation is justified.

Fourth, the number of days a state can be in overdraft has been extended to 14 consecutive working days from 12. In the event of a state's overdraft continuing beyond 14 days, the RBI and its agencies will stop payments.

Finally, the present norm of restricting overdraft to 100 per cent of the normal WMA will continue.

The interest rate on the overdraft will be 3 per cent above the bank rate up to 100 per cent of the normal WMA limit. If the overdraft exceeds the limit, the penal interest rate will be 6 per cent above the bank rate. There was no such penal rate under the current scheme.

Fiscal Reforms

Rationalisation and streamlining of the WMA facility is indeed welcome. But it should be recognised that this is only a small segment of the overall disciplining exercise of state finances. In this context what the *Economic Survey 2002-03* states about the Centre holds true for states too: "Fiscal consolidation continues to remain a major challenge in the process of economic reforms in the country.

Measures taken so far to address the problem of growing fiscal imbalances have not been adequate and commensurate with the magnitude of the problem.

Over the years, the revenue deficit has emerged as the main source of fiscal imbalances with serious implications for public investment and growth of the economy. Current expenditure for exceeding current revenue is the crux of the fiscal and unless this structural deficiency is corrected, other reforms may not be able, by themselves, to restore fiscal health."

It may be recalled here that the Eleventh Finance Commission had recommended a monitorable fiscal reform programme for all states. Fifteen per cent of the revenue deficit grant, meant for 15 states during 2000-05, and a matching contribution by the Centre were to be credited into an incentive fund for distribution as grants for all the 25 states, based on their fiscal performance.

Accordingly, the Government of India had drawn up the states Fiscal Reforms Facility 2000-01 to 2004-05, and an incentive fund of Rs. 10,607 crore was earmarked to encourage States to implement fiscal reform programmes. So far, 18 states have drawn up medium-term programmes in consultation with the Centre. Fiscal reforms cover fiscal consolidation, public enterprise reform, power sector reform, and so on.

While the Centre's Fiscal Responsibility and Budget Management Bill is going through a metamorphosis owing to various proposed amendments, some states have already enacted similar legislation – Karnataka is a case in point. It is wishful thinking to expect states to tighten their belts while the Centre is on a borrowing spree. The Centre's borrowing programme has assumed such alarming proportions that even the Survey admits that it is crowding out the productive sectors of the economy from using the banking sector's resources.

In other words, the bank resources are increasingly being diverted to support government consumption at the cost of supporting the economy's productive sectors.

It would be also not surprising if some states begin to demand as much access to RBI resources as the Centre has. Thus, disciplining state finances is not merely a mechanistic exercise of tightening some facilities such as the WMA. It should be viewed as part of the larger problem of creating a fiscal prudence ethos.

The Hindu Business Line, April 12, 2003.

29

Retail Trade in Government Securities

A Monumental Misadventure

The cacophony of policy pronouncements of savings and investment makes one wonder if there is at all a consistent macromanagement policy of savings. Launching a nationwide securities awareness campaign recently, the Prime Minister made a strong plea for channelling household sector's savings into the stock market to promote equity culture. Most of the household sector's savings, according to him, are now going into less productive non-financial assets and into the banking sector. Instead, if they are channelled into equities, it would facilitate the attainment of the 8 per cent GDP growth target envisaged in the Tenth Plan. It is difficult to understand why bank deposits are clubbed together with less productive investments.

In January, the Finance Minister inaugurated a retail trading system in government securities, by buying Government of India bonds of Rs. 1,000. While these efforts to promote the equity culture and the retail segment of the market in government securities are commendable, a look at the other side of it seems necessary. Both the Y.V. Reddy Committee and the Kelkar Task Force seem to have set out to scuttle small savings in their present form. The former by reducing drastically the returns to small-savings instruments, and the latter by proposing to abolish all fiscal concessions now being extended to small-savings instruments. Building the savings culture is a slow and painstaking process through which India has passed since the latter half of the 1970s, to reach the high phase. Why destroy the existing savings mechanism and try to replace it with an instrument which is anti-savings culture? Government securities, by their very nature, are not the sort of instrument which would appeal to the average saver, both in terms of its reach and returns. The whole exercise of developing the retail segment of the government securities market is, thus, bound to prove to be a monumental misadventure.

Government bonds are securities issued by the Central and State governments. As banker to the Government, the Reserve Bank of India regularly services the payment of interest and the principal on these securities. Since these are sovereign paper, the bonds are regarded as the safest. The other advantages of the government securities are that they are tradeable and can be used as collateral for loans. There is no deduction at source (TDS) on interest payments on government securities. But for individuals, interest income up to Rs. 3,000 per annum is only exempt from income tax.

At present, the participants in the government securities market are usually banks, insurance companies, provident funds and mutual funds. Since the purchase and sale of government securities requires access to the wholesale market, this market has remained out of reach of the individual investors. To facilitate easier access and wider participation in the government securities market, a facility is now being provided to buy and sell government securities through the stock exchanges. The system is analogous to the one available for buying and selling of shares. Keeping in view the interests of small investors, the minimum size of order has been kept low at Rs. 1,000 (face value). Now, any individual can buy or sell government securities in the same manner as buying/selling shares. This would involve three steps. First, the individual would require a demat account with any Depository Participant (DP). Second, he would have to place a buy order for the bonds required with a stock broker. Third, the bonds would be transferred into the individuals demat account, three working days later.

The point in discussing the *modus operandi* of acquiring a government security by a small investor is to underline that notwithstanding the Herculean efforts of the Government and the RBI, government securities cannot be a substitute, or even a near-substitute, for the wide range of small-savings instruments such as National Savings Certificates, Kisan Vikas Patras, or Post-office Savings Bank Deposits. In terms of reach, the post-office and branches of public sector banks have decidedly wider coverage than that of the stock market and brokers. Second, in terms of returns, this is the most inappropriate time to canvass the case of government securities as an alternative investment instrument. The yields in government securities are abysmally low. For instance, the yield on a ten-year bond is lower than 6 per cent. Even the layman knows that Relief Bond 2002, with five-year maturity yield a return of 8 per cent, tax-free. Even bank deposits are more attractive. Third, the element of risk in terms of capital loss. The securities are bought at the market price and, to the extent, the prices go up or down, there is a gain/loss in investing in these securities. The average investor is not equipped to cope with these risks.

It is well-known that last year many public sector banks recorded large 'profits' in treasury operations. This was a by-product of India moving into a very low interest rate regime. If interest rates move up, say, in the next couple of years, the reverse process may start. While institutional investors are equipped to assess and forecast such risks, the small investor is certainly not. Apart from metropolitan cities, how many towns, let alone the villages, have the facility of brokers? How many of even urban investors have a demat account? The track record of the ownership of government securities tells a different story altogether. Why has the RBI not been able to involve institutions other than banks – particularly public sector banks – in investment in government securities? At this stage, it may be recalled that the Narasimham Committee had recommended that the statutory liquidity ratio (SLR) requirement should be reduced from 35 per cent of deposits to 25 per cent. Though the requirement has been reduced for quite sometime, the actual investment deposit ratio today is more than 40 per cent. In other words banks, particularly public sector banks, are bearing the brunt of the government borrowing programme. The RBI has failed to involve institutions other than banks in investment in government securities. Such institutions have the access, the means and the capability to cope with risks and yet they have continued to remain at the periphery of investment in government securities. How much more difficult it would be to involve institutions other than banks in investment in government securities? It may be alright to club bank deposits with less productive investments. But how productive are investments in government securities? There is a structural problem in the case of the Centre's finances: current expenditure exceeds current revenue. In other words, the fiscal problem in respect of the Centre is such that any additional resources that are channellised would go to finance government consumption, rather than investment. Looked at from this angle, the governments efforts to mobilise household sector's resources through retail trading in government securities would result in diverting resources away from productive investments to unproductive investments. It is in this sense that the whole exercise of mobilising household sector's resources assumes the character of a 'misadventure'.

Household sector's savings when invested with banks, as bank deposits, are no less productive than those invested in the stock market through equities. Commercial banks not only provide working capital but also finance medium-term development projects. The preference of equity investment to bank deposits is a hangover of the IMF/World Bank theology. In India, historically commercial banks and development banks have played a far more important role in the development of the economy than the capital market. Even today, the capital market is in a moribund state. On the whole, it is necessary to take a holistic view of the financial sector and encourage the flow of household sector's resources into all productive segments, including banks.

The Hindu Business Line, February 14, 2003.

VII

Hunger, Poverty and Rural Development

Hunger, Poverty and Rural Unemployment

30

Food Distribution and Growth-Equity Linkages

The total quantity of foodgrains with the public sector soared to 62 million tonnes in June 2001, compared to 42 million tonnes a year ago. These stocks are most likely to swell further because the kharif output of foodgrains for 2001-02 has set an all-time record of 106 million tonnes. On the other hand, India continues to be home to the largest absolute number of under-fed and under-nourished people in the world. Thus, semi-starvation and under-nourishment co-exist with the mountain of the so-called "surplus" foodgrains. How does one explain the paradox?

It is time policy-makers of the 1990s, brought up on the diet of IMF/World Bank philosophy of market-led growth, realise that the market does not bring about autonomously a balance between supply of and demand for foodgrains in the Indian context. The mountain of surplus foodgrains is fundamentally different from, say, the mountain of surplus butter in the European community, or surplus wheat in the US, where farmers are compensated for not growing wheat on specific acreages.

In the latter two cases, the domestic demand for butter or wheat has reached a saturation point in the sense that there is no scope for raising domestic demand further.

In sharp contrast, in the Indian case, the surplus is essentially an effective demand surplus in the sense that only the demand for foodgrains of those who can afford to purchase them is met fully. There is enormous potential demand for foodgrains by those who simply do not have the purchasing power to pay for foodgrains; this demand remains unsatisfied. The state is, therefore, required to play a pro-active role by evolving a configuration of policies designed to ensure access to foodgrains by all sections of the population.

The economic justification for wide-spread distribution of foodgrains can be better appreciated if the following three dimensions of growth-equity linkages are highlighted. First, higher growth can be sustained over a period only if growth is widely dispersed.

Second, widespread distribution of foodgrains provides a shortcut to direct and more equitable distribution of income.

The "trickle-down" theory of growth, which postulates that growth generates more employment income and, thus, enables the poor to access foodgrains does not work : even if it does, it is a long haul. The improvement in the quality of life of the bulk of the population, which is the end-objective of all development endeavours, can be achieved directly and quickly by ensuring access to foodgrains by the bulk of the population. Third, there are many other programmes for building human capital through education and health, and so on. The effectiveness of these programmes is contingent upon the adequate provision of foodgrains to the families concerned. Foodgrains, thus, provide the foundation on which other improvement in the quality of life can be built.

An appreciation of these extended dimensions of the growth-equity linkages calls for bold departures from the present insensate approach adopted for foodgrains distribution. The phenomenon of food distribution needs to be treated as analogous to income distribution. Fortunately, we have accumulated an embarrassingly high level of stocks, and can thus bring about the desired distribution-mix.

One of the most important lessons we have learnt is that sustained development should be rooted in process that are socially inclusive. Reinforcing this point, the Nobel Laureate, Prof. Joseph Stiglitz, has emphasized recently that poverty reduction and a more equitable distribution of income have also assumed importance, not only as an end in themselves but also as a means of achieving stronger economic performance. There is ample empirical evidence to show that higher growth was sustained because growth was dispersed widely.

The Asian Tigers, which adopted the objective of "shared growth" in their development strategies, are a concrete example. The draft Approach Paper to the Tenth Plan (2002-2007) seems to have assimilated this growth-equity linkage issue.

"It is important to emphasise that the equity-related objectives of the Plan, which are extremely important, are linked to the growth objective, and the attainment of one may not be possible without the other. For example, high rates of growth are essential if we want to provide a sufficient expansion of sustainable quality employment opportunities to the expanding labour force and ensure a sufficient increase in incomes of the poor and the disadvantaged."

Unfortunately, the assimilation of the principle is not translated into practical measures to promote equality. The mountain of surplus foodgrains, in fact, provides an opportunity to bring about greater equality in income distribution.

While the number of beneficiaries of the public distribution system (PDS) has fallen sharply, the amount of food subsidy has risen, thanks to higher procurement prices and carrying costs. Surplus foodgrains can be converted into an opportunity to achieve a more equitable distribution of income if we can devise appropriate mechanisms to bring about widespread distribution. This can be done through programmes of "Food for Work" or by providing grain loans to cooperatives, NGOs, Self-Help Groups and Panchayati Raj Institutions (*Business Line*, September 21).

The Sampoorna Grameen Rozgar Yojna, launched in September 2001, is no doubt a good beginning. Under this scheme, 50 lakh tonnes of foodgrains worth Rs. 5,000 crore are to be provided every year to states and union territories, free of cost. The programme is designed to generate an additional 100 crore man-days of employment in the rural sector every year.

Welcome as this programme is, it is woefully inadequate to tackle the problem of food security among the poor and the disadvantaged. The utilisation of half of the total stocks of foodgrains, say some 30 million tonnes in the next couple of years, should be the explicit objective of policy. The enormity of the task involved becomes obvious. Only such a massive utilisation of foodgrains meets the test of immediacy.

The problem acquires a sense of urgency because of two factors. First, the immediate need to mitigate large-scale starvation and under-nourishment. This task brooks no delay.

Second, foodgrains are a sort of semi-perishable commodity, deteriorating with the length of storage, especially when the quality of storage is not up to the mark.

Most storage godowns with the Food Corporation of India are small-scale, low-quality structures and some foodgrains are stored in the open, called covered and plinth (CAP), leading to high storage losses, deterioration of quality, and so on. If, therefore, food-grains utilisation has to be massive, the range of rural development works to be undertaken has to be wider micro watershed development projects, road building, afforestation and so on.

Similarly, the task must involve not only the government departments but also voluntary agencies, some of which are already doing excellent work in this sphere, and panchayati raj institutions and cooperative institutions of various types. We must encourage the formation of self-helf group (SHGs) throughout the country, especially in states where food insecurity is high. In fact, *Food Insecurity: Atlas of Rural India*, published by the M.S. Swaminathan Research Foundation, provides an excellent classification of states, indicating the degree of incidence of food insecurity. It, thus, provides a basis for drawing up a blueprint of programmes for utilisation of foodgrains on a massive scale.

Education is, of course, a basic requirement for a meaningful life. Although, today, literacy levels have gone up to 65 per cent, illiteracy continues to be unacceptably high, particularly among women. Hence, a massive programme for Universalisation of Elementary Education (UEE), called the Sarva Shiksha Abhiyan, has been launched, under which about Rs.100,000 crore would be spent till 2010 by the Central and state governments. The programme envisages facilities for school buildings, teachers, teachers' education and academic support, through block and cluster resource centres, girls toilets, textbooks for girls, and so on. The point in giving the details of the programme is to emphasise that an important item — food for poor children, particularly in the rural areas — is missing. Education can not be forced down the throats of starving children. The main issue to drive home is that the effectiveness of such programmes for education and health would be better if access to food-grains is assured. Food security of the poor should be the central focus of society if the quality of life is to improve across sections.

Accumulation of foodgrains of more than 60 million tonnes has been a monumental folly, while the number of beneficiaries of the public distribution (PDS) has fallen and food subsidies are rising.

Viewed in the context of these larger dimensions of foodgrains utilisation, the subject becomes as important as disinvestment or the promotion of foreign direct investment, subjects on which so much of the policy-makers' time and energy is being spent.

The Hindu Business Line, November 27, 2001.

31

WTO

Agricultural Exports and Growth

While signing in 1995 the various agreements under the auspices of WTO there were great expectations. In a liberalised trading environment for agriculture, tariff and non-tariff barriers would come down and fair trading opportunities would open up for all countries including India. Based on these assumptions of substantial reductions in tariff and non-tariff barriers, some studies predicted enormous gains to developing countries including India. These macro models assumed perfectly competitive markets for agricultural commodities. Unfortunately, even after seven years of signing the WTO agreement, an imperfectly competitive export market persists. The Western developed countries have found several escape routes to circumvent the spirit of the WTO agreement and have failed to bring about substantial reduction in domestic and export subsidies in their own countries. Thus, an imperfectly competitive export market structure for agricultural commodities persists and this is the reality with which developing countries have to contend. The emergent scenario is humbling for those market evangelists who had predicted a buoyancy in agricultural exports for developing countries, in the aftermath of the WTO agreement, and had entertained fantasies about agricultural exports acting as an engine of growth for the economy as a whole. Of course, India should exploit such opportunities of export as the existing market offers but this would imply development of small segments of the agricultural sector. The main theme that I would like to develop is that India will have to focus on non-trade and non-price factors to accelerate agricultural growth, bring about rural development in a general and improve the welfare of the rural population. Over the years, though the share of agriculture in total GDP has declined substantially, dependence on agriculture has hardly declined. Agriculture will continue to remain, despite industrialisation and export growth, the main source of livelihood for the bulk of Indian population, for years to come. Hence broad-based agricultural growth, and not enclave growth, should be at the centre of our strategy for rural development and welfare. Larger public investment in rural infrastructure, irrigation, education, extension and health, assume significance in this context. Use of our alarmingly large foodgrains stocks which add up to more than 60 million tonnes for agricultural and rural development is another strategy which needs to be adopted. Of course, focussing on these areas would also strengthen, indirectly India's agricultural export capabilities.

There is a broad consensus that at present globalisation — through WTO in the context of the present discussion — is occurring in a highly inequitable manner and under rules that are biased against developing countries. For instance, global agricultural subsidies are estimated to add up to some $ 360 billion annually, or nearly a billion dollars a day. Of this total, 80 per cent is accounted for by (OECD)[1] countries. Unless domestic and export subsidies are reduced in the developed countries, a fair and just international trade regime in agricultural commodities remains a text-book concept. As Dr. Per Pinstrup-Andersen puts it, "Unless developed countries are willing to open their markets to temperate-zone agricultural exports from developing countries and end tariff escalation against processed and higher value products, however, the benefits that developing countries and the poor people who live in them will derive from globalisation will be limited."

The mention of the emphasis on "non-price factors" is deliberate. In Indian agriculture, supply response to prices is rather poor. Assuming that there is a rise in the export prices of a commodity, it does not automatically ensure larger production of that commodity. Along with price rise, farm technology, extension, credit, and marketing — all these have to lend support to production efforts.

Using of surplus foodgrains to promote rural development and welfare is an area which has not been fully explored. The success of the approach lies in linking utilisation of foodgrains to productive

---

1 Organisation of Economic Cooperation and Development.

activities. The most conspicuous programme which comes to mind is the micro watershed development programme which can be undertaken on a massive scale throughout the country. The bulk of the costs of such programmes would be accounted for by wages which can be paid in kind, namely foodgrains. The technology involved is simple and village panchayats can implement these schemes. The point is that by using surplus foodgrains it will be possible to create additional employment and incomes to the rural poor, at the same time as creating large economic overhead capital. The insurance against drought is another feature of the gain to the economy. Providing food security involves a two-fold objective namely, enlarging availability of foodgrains and providing access to foodgrains. While we have achieved the former, we have yet to achieve the latter. India is home to the largest number of under-fed and under-nourished people in the world. The paradox of the co-existence of a mountain of surplus foodgrains with an alarmingly large number of under-fed population needs to be resolved. Programmes like the micro watershed development programme provide the *modus operandi* to achieve the twin objectives.

Let there be no misunderstanding. I am not expressing "export pessimism" in the neo-classical sense. All that I am seeking to drive home is that given the unwillingness, and not the inability, of developed countries to dismantle their massive domestic support and export subsidies to agriculture in their countries, it would be unrealistic to expect, on the part of India, a major break-through in its agricultural exports.

The thrust of export efforts would have to be highly selective. For instance, India has become a major rice exporter. Indian rice is likely to remain competitive, especially in Asian markets, given the lower freight costs as compared to the US.

In the 1990s, India has increased its exports of both fresh and processed fruits and vegetables, but further expansion in this area would require improvement in infrastructure, storage, transport, processing, and the ability to meet sanitary and technical requirements in developed country markets. Fish exports, where there is also a potential competitive advantage are also conditioned by similar limitations.

In conclusion, it is clear that the key to accelerating agricultural growth and promoting rural welfare lies in the basics — larger public investment in rural infrastructure, irrigation, road, farm technology, extension and so on. The thrust on agricultural exports would have to be highly selective and the impact of agricultural export growth on overall growth in GDP and rural welfare could at best, be marginal.

References

Implications of WTO Agreements for Indian Agriculture (2001), Indian Institute of Management, Ahmedabad.

WTO and Viability of Indian Agriculture (2001), *Economic and Political Weekly*, Mumbai, September 8-14.

Dr. Pinstrup-Andersen (2002), Indian Agriculture in a Globalising World, Exim Bank Mumbai, 2002.

Mujumdar, N.A. (2001), The New Architecture of the Rural Credit System, Mumbai University.

———. (2002), Micro-Credit Institutions, Grain Loans and Rural Development, in Financing Agriculture, April-June.

32

Rural Development

New Perceptions

There was a time when rural development was dismissed as a fancy of the egalitarian romantics. This is no longer so. New perceptions of development economics have resulted in the evolution of what one might call the multifunctional concept of rural development – a concept which should form the core of any meaningful development strategy and not merely an appendage of an independently worked out strategy. Rural development in India seems to hold the key to overall development of the economy, food security and improvement in the quality of life. In the first place I would seek to demonstrate that the 1990s was a lost decade for agriculture and rural development. In the euphoria of liberalisation and globalisation of the Indian economy, agriculture became the Cinderella of Indian policy makers. Blessed were they who debunked the whole philosophy of planned economic development: those who exulted in the alleged miraculous powers of the market-led economy believed that they have began to live in heaven. Economic reforms created an adversarial environment for agricultural growth and rural development. No wonder agricultural growth decelerated sharply. The present decade has inherited the debris of the rural economy shattered by misconceived economic reforms. The mountain of the so-called surplus foodgrains of some 60 million tonnes stands as a monument of the misguided food policy and also of misguided macroeconomic management. Secondly, I would highlight the main elements of the new development economics which focus on equity-linked growth. Thirdly, in the light of the new insights gained into development phenomenon, I would draw a broad sketch of multifunctional concept of rural development and indicate how it is feasible to use the huge foodgrain stocks to create social and economic overhead capital. No sensible economic policy, whether dirigiste or market-led, would have allowed such alarmingly large foodgrains stocks to accumulate in a country which is the abode of the largest number of under fed and under nourished people in the world. The proposal outlined here to utilise a sizeable proportion of foodstocks to create rural employment and generate rural incomes meets the test of "immediacy" in terms of attaining the end-objectives of development, namely, providing food security, reducing poverty, and improving the quality of life.

I. The 1990s: Lost Decade

Alas! It seems that in the 1990s Indian policy makers had not caught up with the new development economics. In the euphoria of liberalisation and globalisation of the Indian economy, to talk of agricultural or rural development became *infra dig*. Financial sector reforms introduced in India in the 1990s were largely mimetic. We have borrowed "Basle Norms" for implementing banking sector reforms, or responded to IMF/World Bank prescriptions as in the case of reforms relating to the development of the capital market. These reforms were "rootless" in the sense that they were not attuned to the India-specific socio-economic milieu. The whole idea appears to have been to replicate an American style financial system in India. The present decade has inherited the debris of the Indian rural economy which was shattered by the mindless pursuit of mimetic policies based on an amateurish understanding of the concept of liberalisation and globalisation. The 1990s was a lost decade for agriculture and rural development generally. The shrinkage of the flow of resources to the rural sector, a misconceived interest rate policy which discriminated against agriculture, a moribund rural credit delivery system, the emergence of a new banking culture, nurtured by reforms, which is far from friendly to agriculture and rural development, and a serious set back to rural employment expansion — all these form part of the debris. No wonder that agricultural growth decelerated sharply: the average annual growth of agricultural GDP in value added terms declined from 3.5 per cent in the 1980s to 2.8 per cent in the 1990s. The last two years 1999-2000 and 2000-2001 were particularly dismal with growth rates of 1.3 per cent and (-)0.2 per cent, respectively. Since I have analysed in-depth the impact of economic reforms on the rural sector elsewhere[1], I would be content here with merely sketching the broad contours of these developments.

We seem to be distancing ourselves from the objective of poverty alleviation, perhaps on the mistaken belief that in a market-led economy, the poor must fend for themselves. It has become fashionable to argue that Government intervention in economic affairs should be minimal. It is against the background that all concessional lending rates to small farmers, or small borrowers generally, were abolished. In the resultant anarchy of interest rates structure, today a small farmer pays an interest rate of 12 per cent on his borrowings from banks – a rate which is decidedly higher than the effective interest rate of 4 or 5 per cent which multinational corporates (MNCs), other corporate elites, and exporters pay. The flow of credit to priority sectors, which include agriculture and small scale industries was below the targeted level of 40 per cent of net bank credit for most of the years in the 1990s. So also was credit to agriculture which was below the prescribed level of 18 per cent of net bank credit. Reserve Bank of India (RBI) winked at these defaults by banks. Although the priority sector credit has been restored to the targeted level in more recent years, credit to agriculture continues to be below the targeted level. Public investment in agriculture shrank.

Thus, the size of the flow of financial resources to agriculture, both in terms of long-term capital and working capital declined sizably, ironically at a phase when the financial system was highly liquid. The Indian economy was so affluent in foreign exchange resources as to afford to promote gold imports to an alarmingly high level of 87 billion in 1998-99. In a capital-starved economy like that of India, macroeconomic policies should be so designed that utilisation of forex results in improved productive capacity and export potential of the economy. Gold imports do neither. The only result is that in the metropolitan and other bigger towns today, there are perhaps more jewellery shops than grocery shops. When it comes to larger investment in irrigation, the same policy makers pleaded paucity of resources, as an excuse. What an amazing perversion of priorities!

---

1 *The New Architecture of the Rural Credit System*, University of Mumbai, August 2001, and *Financial Sector Reforms & India's Economic Development*, Vol. I and II, Academic Foundation, Delhi, 2002.

The moribund rural credit delivery system was part of the debris inherited from the 1990s. Most of the rural branches of Public Sector Banks (PSBs), Regional Rural Banks (RRBs), and cooperative credit institutions were making losses. They had lost the elan of the 1970s or 1980s. Yet another disturbing feature of the system was the new banking culture nurtured by reforms, which laid emphasis on a "quick kill", rather than on promoting growth by extending medium and long-term credit support to the productive sectors of the economy. To give one such example, banks had enough resources to extend bridge loans to enterprises like the M.S. Shoes but they had no funds to support the production of sugar in Maharashtra. The involvement of some PSBs in the securities scam and the more recent involvement of some cooperative banks in the government securities scam, reflect the impact of the new banking culture on their basic approach to banking business.

Finally, rural employment – looking at the preliminary 1999-2000 National Sample Survey (NSS) estimates on employment, many economists had warned that rural employment had suffered a serious setback during the decade of economic reforms. These fears have now been confirmed. I can do no better than quote from a scholarly paper published recently by Chadha and Sahu: "With the release of the final estimates, and adoption of a few methodological refinements, it is now clear that the initial assessment was not wrong.... in our assessment, the overall situation during the post, compared with the pre-reform period does pose signs of concern.[2]

There is also some euphoria about the growth of rural non-farm employment which needs to be tempered. The nature of such employment has to be scrutinised to find out whether it is growth-led or distress-induced.[3] Especially the self-employed sector shelters sizeable disguised unemployment, as the seminal article by Arthur Lewis, "Economic Development with Unlimited Supply of Labour" spelt out long ago. In some cases, self-employment is an apology for employment. It is therefore dangerous to be led by statistical numbers of self-employment alone.

---

2 Economic and Political Weekly (May 28-31, 2002), G.K. Chadha and P.P. Sahu, *Post-Reform Setbacks in Rural Employment*.

3 Indian Journal of Agricultural Economics, (April-June 1998) G. Parthasarathy and others, *Determinants of Rural Non-Agricultural Employment: The Indian Case*.

II. Changing Landscape of Development

Before we get down to the India-specific issues, let us take a brief look at the changing landscape of development economics itself. Over the last fifty years, the approach to development economics has undergone a sea change, shifting from a narrow focus on macroeconomic stabilisation and liberalisation, to a comprehensive framework encompassing all aspects of the economy including social and environmental issues and poverty reduction. Poverty reduction has been brought back to the centre stage of development. One of the most important lessons learnt from development experience is that growth does not trickle down; development must address human needs directly. The second lesson is that sustained development should be rooted in the processes that are socially inclusive.

Reinforcing this point Joseph Stiglitz has emphasised that poverty reduction and a more equitable distribution of income have also assumed an importance not only as an end in themselves but also as a means of achieving stronger economic performance. In fact, the experience of Asian Tiger clearly demonstrates that "Shared growth" is sustainable growth. India's objective should therefore be to promote broad-based and not enclave growth. Even those citadels of the market philosophy – the IMF and the World Bank – have incorporated this approach into their operations. To quote the IMF Managing Director, "Specifically, we have firmly established poverty as a permanent and pressingly urgent matter on the agenda of the international financial community, no longer an issue to be consigned to an after-thought in communiques or policy papers. We have brought these concerns to the heart of our operations. And, equally, we have recognised that poverty and social justice are key ingredients of the framework for national policy formulation". Not to be left behind, the World Bank President has made a more fundamental statement that the Bank's "Core mandate is to reduce poverty". The current development thesis adumbrates that economic dependence, disempowerment, and lack of access to credit are the major causes of poverty. The poor must therefore have their own organisation to become empowered through self-help groups (SHGs) or microcredit institutions. State intervention to improve literacy, skills and health is welcome, but by itself it cannot raise and sustain income-earning capabilities of the poor. Support of credit and other services is essential. The main idea in focussing on these new perceptions of development is to sound a note of warning to the Indian evangelists of the market theology that we cannot afford to ignore the primordiality of the poverty theme; all policies including financial, monetary, and food policies must be anchored in the objective of promoting faster growth specifically designed to reduce poverty.

III. Multi-functional Concept

Viewed against this background of the new perceptions of what development is all about – perceptions which take into account the larger concerns of life beyond the mere growth objective, rural development becomes multifunctional. In fact, in economies like that of India rural development holds the key to overall development, reduction of poverty, improvement in the nutrition standards and health of the bulk of the population, reduction in the incidence of illiteracy, improvement in the quality of life – all these could be attained through agricultural and rural development.

We have waited for 50 years, since the inception of planning in 1951 to reduce poverty and have failed miserably. We cannot afford to wait for another 50 years to tackle the poverty issue. If China could reduce its poverty to nominal levels in a period of two decades, why not India? In other words, any measures to reduce poverty should be subjected to the test of "immediacy". One sees a ray of hope in the mountain of foodgrains stocks of some 60 million tonnes accumulated with the Food Corporation of India (FCI) – this mountain stands as a monument of our misguided food policy and misguided macro-economic management. India is home to the largest number of under-fed and under-nourished people in the world. How does then one reconcile the co-existence of such a large quantity of the so-called "surplus" foodgrains with an alarming number of under-fed people? The simple answer is that this is not a genuine surplus but an effective demand surplus. A sizeable proportion of the population does not simply have the wherewithal to buy foodgrains. And this, in turn, is due to the fact that the only asset that families in this category have is labour and as we have seen earlier, the economy has failed to generate the adequate quantum of rural employment. Coupled with this fact is the misguided food policy.

In an over-zealous attempt to cut down food subsidies, the Government of India tightened the criteria for eligibility governing access to the public distribution of foodgrains, at the same time as the issue prices were raised successively. As a cumulative impact of these misguided policies, off-take of foodgrains declined and stocks of foodgrains have soared to such heights. While foodgrains stocks accumulate with FCI, immeserisation of rural masses has driven many to semi-starvation. While stocks accumulate, men decay. The FCI is not exactly known for its efficiency. Inefficient operation, bad and defective storage, deterioration in the quality of foodgrains, wastage – all of these factors have made the carrying costs of foodgrains by FCI heavy. Any sound macro-economic management would never have allowed such large stocks to accumulate in the first place.

The co-existence of the mountain of foodgrains and the mass of unemployed rural labour is a unique situation specific to the current Indian scenario. It seems feasible to convert this situation into an opportunity to trigger higher rural growth, create additional rural employment and income, and build additional social and economic overhead capital. The basic idea is to establish a grain loan facility which is accessible to all those involved in rural development — financial institutions, like commercial banks, regional rural banks (RRBs) and all cooperative credit institutions, microcredit institutions, village panchayats, NGOs and self-help groups (SHGs). The FCI should immediately earmark a sizeable proportion of its foodgrain stocks, say 10 million tonnes, for utilising them as working capital, as it were, and begin to extend the grain loans to the eligible institutions, on a deferred payments basis. The interest rate should be nominal at, say, 1 per cent and the repayment could start after a period of, say, 5 years. The receiving institution could add a small margin of, say, one-half of one per cent and on-lend to the final beneficiary. The modalities of how the FCI could extend grain loans to a federal institutions, say, a Central Cooperative Bank at the district level, and the price at which grains should be valued, the procedures of repayment to be followed by the final borrower, that is NGOs or SHGs or the Panchayat - all these need to be worked out for different states.

Such a grain loan facility confers a two-fold benefit. First, FCI's carrying costs which are rising because of the factors mentioned earlier, would be greatly reduced. Second, the resources of credit institutions involved as intermediaries in the whole transaction would be substantially enhanced. Their own incomes would also rise because of the larger turnover.

The real test of the success of the grain loan facility lies in linking utilisation of grain loans to productive activities. The most conspicuous programme which comes to mind in this context is the micro watershed development programme which can be undertaken on a massive scale throughout the length and breadth of the country. The bulk of the costs of such programmes would be accounted for by wages, which can be paid in kind through grains obtained from the FCI. The net gains to the economy in terms of insurance against drought, availability of drinking water throughout the year, higher rural employment and incomes — all these far out-weigh any notional losses which FCI may suffer by extending grain loans on a deferred payments basis. Social forestry is another programme which fits into this framework. There may be other programmes which are location-specific to the regions concerned. Each state could identify such programmes which could be largely financed by grain loans.

If the reach of such loans is to be widened, through the instrumentality of financial institutions, the need to streamline the rural credit delivery system becomes obvious. The existing network needs to be strengthened to make it vibrant. Similarly, the network of NGOs, SHGs and Micro Credit Institutions needs to be widened greatly. The snail's pace at which NABARD is at present expanding SHGs would not do. A massive expansion of these institutions is an ineluctible necessity.

The existence of a mountain of foodgrains thus provides an excellent opportunity to promote rural development, through the instrumentality of financial institutions, NGO, SHGs and panchayati raj institutions (PRIs).

There is yet another reason why rural or agricultural growth becomes central to overall growth. If the objective is to put the Indian economy into the orbit of higher growth trajectory of 8 per cent, as the current discussions on the Tenth Plan indicate, this can be achieved only on the basis of a buoyant agriculture which can grow at around 4 per cent. Public investment in irrigation, extension services, adequate flow of credit, both short-term and long-term — all these would have to become the essential ingredients of policy.

Fortunately, wisdom seems to have dawned at last on our policy-makers in the current decade and one hopes that agriculture will cease to be the Cinderella. The Union Budget for 2000-01 embodies the following aphoristic statement of the Finance Minister "It is my firm belief that sustained and broad-based growth of agriculture is essential for alleviating poverty, generating incomes and employment, assuring food security and sustaining a buoyant domestic market for industry and services". (Budget Speech, 1999-2000). Resurruction of agricultural growth or rural development in general is the best thing that could have happened to the Indian economy. In a similar vein, the new development economics also seems to have percolated to the architects of the Tenth Plan: "It is important to emphasise that the equity-related objectives of the Plan which are extremely important are intimately linked to the growth objective and attainment of one may not be possible without the attainment of the other. For example, high rates of growth are essential if we want to provide a sufficient expansion of sustainable high quality employment opportunities to our expanding labour force and ensure a sufficient increase in incomes of the poor and the disadvantaged" (Draft Approach Paper to the Tenth Five Year Plan (2002-2007), page 5). However, the planner should not be content with merely making appropriate noises. One looks in vain for concrete programmes in the Plan document specifically designed to translate this approach into concrete reality.

Finally, there is one India-specific issue, which reflects the broader concerns of life and which has not received the attention it deserves. This is what one may call building the development conscience. Contemporary Indian society is plagued by moral pollution and it is time that social scientists address this issue. This poses a more dangerous threat to development than, say, environmental pollution which has attracted a good deal of attention, both nationally and internationally. The rampant corruption, including frequent scams in the financial sector, erosion of medical ethics, irregularities in the academic field, for example, the erratic teaching habits of some primary school teachers who may stay in towns and "visit" their village school only occasionally, marks – tampering at higher levels of education, and promotions based on considerations other than merit. Similar irregularities exist in the health-care sphere also – primary health centres may have regular offices in the village and paramedics regularly drawing by their salaries but these centres are rarely open for actual treatment. Again, take the case of fiscal termites: about one-third of electricity consumption is not "billed" but treated as "transmission and distribution losses". How can any development plan, howsoever well designed, succeed in such an environment?

There is thus a need to build development conscience among all sections of the population. From times immemorial, Indian philosophy has maintained that the all-round development of the society is best achieved through the betterment of the individual and this concept of betterment of individual includes, economic well-being but extends beyond it. Social conscience must be inculcated through educational and professional training. We must be sensitised to the abject poverty, the squalor, disease, ignorance and illiteracy that surround us and we must begin to think in terms of what is our *dharma* or duty towards alleviating some of the infirmities that afflict our compatriots. The building up of development conscience would go a long way towards improving economic growth and also evolving a compassionate society.

Chinese Example

A word about the Chinese example. The Chinese growth experience since it introduced reforms in 1978 is illuminating, because of the comparability of economic situation in India in terms of population pressure and poverty levels. Perhaps, more important in the present context is the fact that China pursued its own financial policies, with the help of its own institutions, however imperfect they might have been. China did not ape IMF/World Bank prescriptions nor did it try to adopt the so-called "international best practices" with which RBI seems to be obsessed. Indian evangelists of the market philosophy should note that reforms in China proceeded despite the lack of complete market liberalisation and privatisation. Over the two decades from 1978 to 1998, agricultural GDP grew at the phenomenal rate of 5.2 per cent per annum, and rural industrial output at 3.1 per cent. There was an explosion of non-farm employment. Rural industry grew steadily employing about 25 per cent of the total rural labour force. Township and Village Enterprises expanded rapidly during the reform era, contributing about 40 per cent to the total industrial output. Access to credit, subsidized credit at that, was one of the important factors which facilitated such rapid growth. The reduction in poverty levels was miraculous; in 1997 poverty was limited to only six per cent of the rural population.

Conclusion

The existence of the mountain of surplus foodgrains provides an excellent opportunity to promote rural development, through the instrumentality of financial institutions, NGOs and SHGs. Grain loan seems to be an ideal vehicle through which this can be achieved. In fact, the case for widespread distribution of foodgrains among all sections of the population has much wider ramifications. Designing a configuration of policies aimed at ensuring access to foodgrains by all sections of the population should form part of the macro-economic management. Equity-linkages are the end-objective of development, namely, an improvement in the quality of life.

This is the edited version of the special Lecture given on 22nd June, 2002, at Dharwad, on the occasion of D.P. Karmarkar Birth Centenary.

Economic & Political Weekly, September 28, 2002.

33

Eliminate Hunger Now, Poverty Later

An assortment of fragmented academic profundities does not add up to a holistic and pragmatic policy package. Take the following statements. First, the Mid-Year review of the economy, presented by the Ministry of Finance to Parliament on December 3, makes the point that we are surplus in rice and wheat but there is a sizeable shortage of pulses and oilseeds.

The review finds fault with the minimum support price (MSP) system, implying that support prices for rice and wheat should be reduced and raised for pulses and oilseeds. No one questions the rationale underlying the Ministry's statement.

The moot point is, why did it take three years for this truth to dawn on the Ministry? Public sector foodgrains stocks rose to 29 million tonnes in 1999-2000 — well above the buffer stock norm of 21 million tonnes. The stocks rose further to 44 million tonnes in 2000-01, and soared to 63 million tonnes in June 2002.

The Ministry also lacks a sense of history as to the critical role played by the MSP system to boost the production of rice and wheat to the present comfortable levels. Second, the fiscal deficit of the Centre is growing and subsidies need to be cut.

Hence, subsidies on rice and wheat were cut and the issue prices of both rice and wheat, distributed through the Public Distribution System (PDS), were raised substantially. Result : the off-take of foodgrains from the PDS fell sharply from some 26 million tonnes in 1996-97 to below 18 million tonnes in 2000-01. With successively good agricultural years, the size of procurement went on rising and the net result was the soaring of stocks to today's embarrassingly high level of more than 60 million tonnes.

Third, these are the heydays of privatisation. The Government must reduce its involvement in economic activities. Hence, during the

1990s, public investment in agriculture and related rural development activities declined sharply. The net addition to irrigated area, for instance, was the lowest during this decade. This is not because of the shortage of resources.

We are rich enough to afford to import gold worth $7 billion annually, but we have no resources to invest in irrigation. This decline in public investment in the rural sector has had a serious adverse impact on rural employment, thereby reducing the rural demand for foodgrains. This factor also contributed to the swelling of foodgrains stocks with the public sector.

The three policy measures discussed above cannot be faulted in terms of micro decisions but, cumulatively, they have led to a macro mess. The mountain of public sector foodgrains of more than 60 million tonnes in an economy, which is the abode of the largest number of under fed and under nourished people in the world, stands as a monument to macroeconomic mismanagement.

Utilisation of the mountain of surplus foodgrains is the gravest single problem facing the economy today.

Fortunately, the answer to this question was provided by the three distinguished experts at the 62nd Annual conference of the Indian Society of Agricultural Economics held at Delhi during December 19-21, 2002; Dr. C. Rangarajan, in his inaugural address, Dr. G.K. Chadha, in his Presidential Address, and Dr. Y.K. Alagh, in his special lecture.

Piecing together the strands of thought of these three experts, one could formulate the following proposition: in the present circumstances Dr. Alagh put forward the proposal that, in the present circumstances, it is feasible to tackle the problem of elimination of hunger first, the elimination of poverty can take place later. Analytically, this is an important step forward towards evolving what might be described as the "second best" solution. Conventional wisdom stipulates that the problem of poverty can be tackled through higher GDP growth, employment expansion and additional generation of income. But this process is a long haul and may take at least two decades.

However, in the unique situation in which the economy is placed today, without waiting for two decades, the problem of hunger can be solved because we have surplus foodgrains of more than 60 million tonnes. Besides, the country's foreign exchange reserves have also reached a new peak of nearly $68 million in December 2002.

If need be, the country can afford to import any supplementary food items such as pulses and edible oil. After all, the end-objective of all development endeavours is to improve the quality of life of the bulk of the population. And what better method can there be than the nearly total elimination of hunger to achieve this end-objective?

It is time, contemporary policy-makers sit up and take notice of this strategy. The proposed strategy also passes the test of 'immediacy' in the sense that elimination of hunger can be achieved here and now.

Before discussing the *modus operandi* of utilisation of foodgrains surplus for elimination of hunger, a word about the minimum support price (MSP) system. It is now fashionable among policy-makers to debunk the MSP and the associated paraphernalia such as the procurement and storage of foodgrains by the Food Corporation of India. State intervention in foodgrains trade is a dirty word in today's lexicon.

These critics lack a sense of history. In fact, MSP and the associated paraphernalia form part of the mechanism which transformed India from a chronically food-deficit economy into a food-surplus economy. The grim food situation in the pre-Green Revolution period when India was dependent on American food aid under PL480 is portrayed in the following passage, quoted by Dr. Chadha, from the book *Famine 1975* authored by Paddock Brothers.

"The US will have to apply the classical medical 'triage' method. Like doctors in the battlefield trying to make the best use of minimum resources, it will have to decide which countries to save and which to sacrifice.

Today, India absorbs like a blotter 25 per cent of the entire US wheat crop. No matter how one may adjust present statistics and allow for future increases in the US wheat crop, it will be beyond the resources of the US to keep famine out of India during the 1970s.

Reason : of all the national leaderships, the Indian comes close to being the most childish and inefficient and perversely determined to cut the country's economic throat. The moral: if other more deserving countries are to be saved, India must be sacrificed."

To this, Dr. Alagh added the Hudson Institute's statement made at about the same time: "Indian cannot feed its million and the world cannot feed India."

It is a tribute to the Indian planners, agricultural scientists, extension workers and the whole range of administrators whose concerted efforts transformed India into a food surplus economy. Foodgrains production has risen from 50 million tonnes in 1950 to 210 million tonnes today. The average Indian farmer may be illiterate but his practicality and earthiness, are well documented.

The remarkable response of the farmer to the Green Revolution is too well known to need elaboration.

The immediate need is to impart some purpose to the foodgrains mountain. The FCI should establish a "grain loan facility", under which all those institutions engaged in agricultural and rural development could obtain, as a loan, rice and wheat from the FCI to support the development activities (*Economic and Political Weekly*, September 26, October 4, 2002).

These institutions include co-operatives, RRBs, micro-credit institutions, NGOs engaged in rural development and self-help groups (SHGs). It would thus help to generate sizeable rural employment and support a wide range of rural development activities. Thus, panchayati raj institutions engaged in micro watershed development or afforestation activities can benefit from this facility. This alone would go a long way towards eliminating hunger in the rural sector.

In addition, through a system of food grants, it should be possible to organise community kitchens in vulnerable areas to feed school-going children and destitutes. Such activities could be part of the social security system.

The apprehensions about such grain loans and grants, resulting in the enlargement of the Centre's budget deficit, are baseless. Utilisation of surplus foodgrains in such a manner does not mean injection of primary money in the economy and, hence, the additional budget deficit is non-inflationary. The enlargement of the Centre's deficit would be only notional and, in that sense, it is a "below the line" deficit.

While the conventional methods of elimination of poverty through higher GDP growth and expansion of employment may continue to be pursued, a well-thought-out mechanism must be devised to eliminate hunger by utilising the mountain of surplus foodgrains.

The Hindu Business Line, January 8, 2003.